AMERICAN SILVER

Paul Revere as portrayed (c. 1765) by his friend and patron, John Singleton Copley. The inverted pear-shaped teapot is ready to be engraved and flat-chased with the nearby tools

AMERICAN SILVER

John Marshall Phillips

DOVER PUBLICATIONS, INC.
Mineola, New York

Bibliographical Note

This Dover edition, first published in 2001, is an unabridged republication of the work originally published in 1949 by Chanticleer Press Inc., New York. For this reprint, the color plates from the 1949 edition are reproduced in color on the inside covers, as well as in black and white in their original positions within the book.

Library of Congress Cataloging-in-Publication Data

Phillips, John Marshall, 1905–1953.
American silver / John Marshall Phillips.
p. cm.
Originally published: New York : Chanticleer Press, 1949.
Includes bibliographical references.
ISBN 0-486-41817-0 (pbk.)
1. Silverwork—United States. I. Title.

NK7112 .P5 2001
739.2'3773—dc21

2001028842

Manufactured in the United States of America
Dover Publications, Inc., 31 East 2nd Street, Mineola, N.Y. 11501

CONTENTS

SCHAATS

COLOR PLATES*

Frontispiece

Paul Revere (1735–1818), by John Singleton Copley

Plate II

Two-handled Covered Cup, 1744, by Jacob Hurd

Plate III

Eighteenth-century Gold: Spoon and Bells by Jacobus van der Spiegel
Teaspoons and Strainer Spoon by Simeon Soumain
Necklace by Peter van Dyck; "Freedom Box" by Samuel Johnson
Rattle by Daniel Christian Fueter

Plate IV

Nathaniel Hurd by John Singleton Copley

*For this edition, the color plates are reproduced in color on the inside covers, as well as in black and white in their original positions within the book.

HULL AND SANDERSON

BLACK AND WHITE PLATES

The author is grateful to the following collectors and institutions for permission to reproduce items from their collections:

Mark Bortman (*Pl.*30); Mrs. Maurice Brix (*Pl.*17a); the Cleveland Museum of Art (*Pl.* IV); Dartmouth College (*Pl.*21a); First Parish Church, Dorchester, Mass. (*Pl.*9); Mrs. Lloyd K. Garrison (*Pl.*16a); Mrs. George A. Goss (*Pl.*8a); Harvard University (*Pl.*12); Edward J. Holmes (*Pl.*8b); Independence Hall, Philadelphia (*Pl.*24b); Mr. & Mrs. Walter M. Jeffords (*Pls.* 18b, 24a); the Massachusetts Historical Society (*Pl.*29); the Metropolitan Museum of Art, New York (*Pls.* 15, 20b); the Museum of Fine Arts, Boston, Mass. (*Pls.* I, 3b, 4b, 21b, 26); Yale University (*Pls.* II, III, 1, 2a, 2b, 3a, 4a, 5, 6a, 7, 10b, 10c, 11, 13, 14, 16b, 17b, 17c, 18a, 19, 20a, 22, 23, 25a, 25b, 27a, 28, 31, 32).

Photographs by: Yale University Art Gallery (*Pls.*1–3a, 4a–9, 10b–14, 16b–20a, 21a, 22–24a, 25a, 25b, 27a–29, 31, 32); the Museum of Fine Arts, Boston, Mass. (*Pls.*I, 3b, 10a, 21b, 26, 30); the Metropolitan Museum of Art, New York (*Pls.*15, 16a, 20b); the Pennsylvania Historical Society (*Pl.*24b).

ERRATA: Pl. 15, caption: For $9\frac{1}{8}$", read $9\frac{1}{2}$". Pl. 30, caption: For $5\frac{5}{16}$", read $5\frac{15}{16}$". Pl. II caption: Insert *Height* $15\frac{1}{8}$". Bibliography: For Pleasants, G. Hall, read Pleasants, J. Hall.

GRIGNON

Chapter one

The Silversmith

So long as brass, so long as books endure,
So long as neat wrought pieces thou'rt secure.
Thomas Flatman (1674).

BY THE MIDDLE OF THE SEVENTEENTH CENTURY, DETERMINED AND venturesome peoples, mainly of English and Dutch descent, had established permanent homes in the seaport villages which had sprung up along the Atlantic seaboard. The natural resources together with the geographic location of these villages and the heritage of their inhabitants largely determined their economic life. As the people of both nations had been bred in a seafaring tradition, it was natural that they should turn their attention to the pursuit of trade and commerce. The trade pattern established by Boston, the largest and most important colonial port during the seventeenth century, also characterized other ports. As early as 1670 merchant ships were to be found trading with the West Indies, the Portuguese islands, English and English-known continental ports as well as with the neighboring coastal towns. The result of this active commercial expansion was an influx of English, Dutch, French, Mexican, Portuguese and Spanish coin, which in a day of no banks created a security problem. Theft of money and plate, as silverware was then commonly known, is one of the crimes most frequently recorded in the surviving court records of that era. They continued despite such a harsh penalty as that imposed on Thomas Streatchley of Swansey who in 1681 was convicted of stealing plate valued at £3 18s. and was sentenced to fifteen stripes at the whipping post and a fine of £8. If the fine was not paid in one month, the complainant was free to sell the convicted man.

The difficulty of securing coins, and the even greater problem of proving ownership in the event of their being stolen or lost, created a place for the silversmith in the community. At a comparatively small cost he could melt the coins, forge and hammer them into objects for use or display, which by means of form, size, engraved decoration or maker's mark, could be readily identified in event of loss or theft. How this worked is illustrated by the following advertisements in our early colonial newspapers:

Stollen on Saturday the 4 currant, from Mrs. Susanna Campbell, Widow in Boston, A Silver Tankard that holds about two Wine Quarts, has Sir Robert Robinson's Coat of Arms engraven on the forepart of it, wherein are three ships, and the Motto in Latin. Whoever can give any true Intelligence of the same, so as that the Owner may have it again, shall be sufficiently rewarded. [*Boston News-Letter*, Nov. 6/13, 1704.]

Taken out of the House of Mr. Edward Eastham who keeps the Fighting Cocks-Inn in New York, a Silver Quart Tankard, marked on the Handle $\overset{E}{ES}$ engraven, the Silversmith's Mark is $\underset{B}{WK}$ Punch'd, and a cypher on the Lid of E S. The Person who is suspected to have taken it is of middle Stature, wore his own dark coloured Hair or a natural Wig, and a brown Coat with a small Cape, very much worn, and out at the Elbows. Three Pounds as a Reward to anyone that shall bring the said Tankard home, and no Questions asked. If left in secure Hands the Reward shall be paid on Receipt of the Tankard. If offered to be sold or pawn'd pray stop it. N.B. He passes by the name of John Coffin. [*The New York Weekly Journal*, May 24, 1736.]

The popularity of the silversmith's craft was further increased as a result of the inflation caused in the early eighteenth century in the colonies by the emission of Bills of Credit. The following prices of silver taken from a memorandum, from the books of the Boston goldsmiths, Jacob Hurd and Thomas Edwards, covering the period 1700–1753, made in the latter year by Ezra Stiles, while a tutor at Yale, are very enlightening. In 1700 silver was valued at 7 shillings per ounce; by 1710 it had advanced to 8s.; 1714, 9s.; 1722, 14s.; 1733, 23s.; 1744, 34s.; 1749, 60s.; 1750, 56–50s.; 1751–53, 50s. As a result of such price fluctuation, the rich and cautious merchant, who hoped to preserve and increase his estate, was more apt to patronize the local silversmith than to send his coin abroad. Sending it abroad also involved risk of capture by the pirates and privateers who infested the waters.

The use of plate, both large and small, as pledge and even as payment for real estate is recorded in our colonial archives. In 1746 when Nathaniel Hempstead of New London sought to borrow money from his grand-father, the canny Joshua Hempstead records in his Diary that he lent him "so much Silver Money as his Silver Spoon weighs and took ye spoon for security." Some years earlier, when the Deacons of the Reformed Church at Albany bought a piece of land adjoining the Church pasture, they paid the several grantors at the rate of 90 guilders each, in plate. This particular transaction affords an interesting commentary upon values as well as the source of raw material in 1700. Each grantor received a silver cup made of 6 heavy pieces of eight valued at 81 guilders by the Albany silversmith, Koenraet Ten Eyck, who was paid at the rate of 9 guilders per cup for the fashioning, making a total of 90 guilders. As a result of this economically created demand for plate and the survival of the mediaeval apprenticeship system, silver became the first of the arts to flourish in the New World.

The skill of the silversmith was based upon the apprenticeship system established in England in the thirteenth century and subject to well-defined regulation, especially during Elizabeth's reign, by the Worshipful Company of Goldsmiths of the City of London; the Company was responsible, then as now, for maintaining the quality of manufactured wares of gold and silver as well as coin of the realm. Transplanted to the colonies, this system assured the artisan of successors and provided him with a supply of skilled labor. Under the terms of the indenture, made before a County Court, the apprentice was bound at the age of fourteen to serve a master craftsman for a period of seven years. In those days this was the only means of advancement in one's chosen craft. In 1660 the Selectmen of Boston voted that no person could open a shop who was not twenty-one years of age and could not present evidence from town records of a full seven years' service as an apprentice. The same ruling applied in New York City by 1675, following the taking-over of its government by the British. The indenture stipulated that the apprentice live in his Master's house, serve him faithfully, obey his lawful commands, keep his secrets (trade) and protect his interests, promise not to absent himself from the Master's house save with his permission, not to frequent ale houses, etc. The Master in turn was bound to provide sufficient meat, drink and washing in winter time fitting for an apprentice and to suffer the apprentice to attend the winter evening school, usually at his father's expense, and to teach him the art or mystery of a Goldsmith, the popular name for a worker in the precious metals.

For the average impressionable young apprentice, the mysteries of the craft became a part of his daily life. He became familiar with all the steps in the fashioning of an object from the melting of the coins, the forging of the sheet, the raising of the form, the casting of small separate parts, assembling and soldering them, to the chasing, polishing and engraving of the finished object. This familiarity developed in him a feeling for the metal, the forms into which it could be worked, its appropriateness to its use, and a sense of balance and proportion.

In those days before pattern books and specialization, the silversmith was not only a designer but also an artisan, skilled in the handling of a great variety of tools. One of the most interesting and revealing lists known to the writer occurs in the inventory of the estate of Richard Conyers, a London-trained goldsmith who was made a freeman of the Worshipful Company of Goldsmiths of the City of London in 1689, was elected to its Livery in 1694, and emigrated to Boston in the late seventeenth century.

The tools were appraised by two fellow craftsmen, Boston-trained Jeremiah Dummer and London-trained Edward Webb.

An Inventory of the Estate of Richard Conyers, Late of Boston Goldsmith Dec'ed Taken and Apprized by the Subscribers the 4th Day of April 1709

	£	s.	d.		£	s.	d.
1 Large forging Anvill				9 Raising Anvills			
268 lb. at /10$^{s.}$ p lb.	10	3	8	172 lb. at 10: 1 Broke	7	3	9

	£	s.	d.
1 Large planishing Teast			
58½ lb. D°·	2	8	9
1 Spoon Teast			
29 lb. at 12 D°·	1	9	0
4 Spoon Punches			
15¼ lb. at 10		12	8
7 Stakes			
27 lb. at D°·	1	2	6
1 Skillet & Ingott			
29½ lb. at D°·	1	4	7
1 Large Vice			
22 lb. at 9d		16	6
3 Forging hammers		7	6
25 Small hammers	1	5	0
1 Ring Swage		3	6
1 Clasp Stamp		4	0
1 Tankard Swage		1	0
12 Cuting punches		10	0
6 Dapping punches		3	0
1 pr. Flasks		10	0
3 per Sheers		3	0
4 pr. Hand Vices		5	0
5 pr. Plyers		5	0
2 pr. Nealing Tongs		2	0
2 pr. holding Tongs		2	0
1 pr. Casting Tongs		2	0
1 pr. Drawing Tongs		2	0
1 Drawing Bench		5	0
1 pr. Large Bellows	1	10	0
1 pr. hand Bellows		2	0
1 pr. Screw plates		5	0
2 Engines for Swages		10	0
3 pr. Compasses		4	0
2 Iron Triblets		1	6
Old files 4 lb.		2	0
2 Gravers		4	0
1 cuting Chissell		1	0
1 Nurling Iron		1	0
3 Old Brass pans			
26 °· at /12	1	6	0

	£	s.	d.
2 Copper pans			
6¾ at 2		13	6
Old Brass patterns			
17½ at /10		14	7
3 pr. Scales		12	0
3 pr. Brass Weights			
12 °·		15	0
1 pile of Weights			
48 oz.		5	0
1 Sett of Small Weights			
4 lb.		6	0
1 Button Stamp	1	0	0
9 training Weights		3	0
Glass case		10	0
2 Burnishing Stons		2	0
Old Cast Brass			
60½ lb. at /6	1	10	3
3 Bell Weights			
480 oz.	1	0	0
1 Pile old Weights			
256 oz.		10	0
5 anvils Ws.			
100 oz. at /10	4	3	4
2 Ditto			
13 oz.		10	10
4 Small Teasts & Swages			
54 °· at /6	1	7	0
6 Spoon Punches 4 Stakes			
39 °· at /8	1	6	0
17 Cuting Punches			
at 8 per pr.		5	8
27 Dapping Punches			
45 °· /8	1	10	0
1 pr. of Large Stock Sheers			
28½		19	0
3 pr. hand Sheers		3	0
12 forging hammers			
87 at 7	2	10	9
25 Small hammers		18	0
3 Drawing Irons		2	0

	£	s.	d.
3 Nurling Irons		2	0
1 pestle 1 Ingott 1 Ladle 55 at /3		6	3
1 pr. Small Screw plates		3	0
1 Small Ingott		1	0
1 pr. board vice		2	0
1 pr. Large holding Tongs		2	0
2 Saws		2	0
1 Screw Box		5	0
1 pr. of Large Scales		12	0
2 pr. Small Scales		5	0
1 pr. Nealing Tongs		1	0
1 Iron		2	0
1 pr. Brass Flasks $5\frac{1}{2}$ o.		6	0
1 Glew pott		1	0
1 pr. hand Bellows		2	0
2 Boxes Chassing punches		6	0
15 Canes	1	4	0
15 Sword Blades		15	0
1 Glass Case		2	6
1 Large Raising Anvill 73 o. at /6	1	16	6
1 Large Skillet 42 at 9	1	11	6
9 Rings with Stones and pearls at 10/p	4	10	0
3 Ditto with Large Stones at 6/	2	8	0
1 pr. Gold Earrings with Pearl Drops		12	0

	£	s.	d.
1 Large Stone Ring	1	5	0
1 pr. Stone Earrings Sett in Silver		1	6
1 Gold Ring with Six Small Stons		12	0
2 pr. Stone buckles		6	0
2 Stone Girdle buckles		10	0
1 Olde hatt buckle		1	0
6 pr. Stone buttons		4	0
3 pr. Ditto		3	0
10 Cornelions 1 Chrystall		5	6
10 Glass Necklaces		5	0
5 Ivory Boxes		2	6
Enamell		2	6
A parcell Small pearle		4	0
Large pearle		9	0
— pearle		5	0
1 Lead Stone	1	0	0
2 Bone heads for Canes		4	0
4 Ditto		1	0
1 Knife handle		1	0
1 Watch	2	0	0
1 Silver Tankard 1 Tobacco Box Wt. oz. 36 dwt. 10 at 8/	14	12	0
Seventy-Seven Ounces of Silver in Sundry old & New things in the hands of Thomas Milner at /8 per oz.	30	16	0
4 Chrystalls for Watches	–	–	–
	£126	0	2

While no known pictorial representation of an early American silversmith's shop exists, it is likely that Conyers, in view of his London training, modelled his shop on that shown as a frontispiece to A NEW TOUCH-STONE for Gold and Silver Wares . . . To which is likewise added, The useful and easie TABLES of Mr. *John Reynolds* of the Mint, (with a Key to the same) plainly shewing how to cast up and make all

Plate II

The richness of the metal and beauty of form in the Queen Anne style is enhanced by the finely cast panelled handles and engraved ornamental inscription of this monumental two-handled covered cup by Jacob Hurd, a presentation piece of 1744, honoring an early naval victory in King George's War

sorts of GOLD and SILVER true *Standard* (Plate 1). This treatise, first issued in 1677, was already in its second edition by 1679, three years before Conyers began his London apprenticeship.

Conyers received his silver not in sheets as does the silversmith today but in the form of coins or pieces outmoded in style. In either case his first task was to melt the silver and refine it to true standard and pour it into his *ingott*, then hammer out a sheet on his *large forging anvill* until the required thickness of metal was achieved, depending upon the object to be fashioned. Then cutting with *sheers* a circular piece of flat metal, the diameter of which was equal to the length of the profile line of the piece desired, he inscribed with the *compasses* a series of concentric circles to act as guides for the hammer strokes. As silver becomes brittle under hammering, it was necessary to soften the metal by heating it in a charcoal forge fanned by hand *bellows*. This process is known as annealing and to handle the red-hot silver Conyers used his *nealing tongs*. As the metal hardened, he proceeded to shape the vessel on the *raising anvill*, using a series of hammers, keeping the metal malleable by repeated annealing operations. Such parts as spouts, covers, and handles were made separately and applied. Mouldings were fashioned on the *drawing bench* in the *engines for swages*. Such small parts as handle tips, hinge plates, cover finials, thumbpieces, handles for cups and porringers were cast from *brass patterns* in a specially prepared compact sand held in iron frames known as *flasks*, and although the castings when finished were filed and chased, one still finds the tell-tale grains imbedded in them. Hammer marks in the metal were removed by the *planishing teast*. For relief work in decoration, *chasing punches* and *hammers* were employed to model the surface against the resilient pitch with which the vessel was filled after its sides had been embossed by means of hammering from the inside. The *gravers* were used to sharpen chasing and for the engraving of ornament, initials, cyphers and coats of arms. The handwrought surface with its individual but charming variation was hand-polished with the *burnishing stones*.

The craftsman's final step was to strike his mark on the vessel, thus declaring its quality. The stamp followed the early English practice of having the first initials of the craftsman's given name and surname, sometimes accompanied by a device such as a fleur-de-lys, circle or rose within a shield or reserve. The importance of the silversmith's mark as a means of identification in the case of lost or stolen silver has already been suggested. Its parallel use in distinguishing between pieces for distribution in legacies is indicated by the will of Samuel Winckley of Portsmouth, drawn in 1726, in which there are references to "a silver Porringer made by Mr. Dummer, two silver Canns wth my Name on Them & Made by Mr. Tyler, two large silver porringers & one silver Can Mark S W: & the Goldsmiths mark in Each I:R: Silver Tankard made by Mr. Greenough, six silver spoons made by Mr. Cunny, a Silver Spoone Made by Danll Greenough." Early in the second quarter of the eighteenth century, the silversmith often used his full surname preceded by his initial such as J. HURD in a reserve or rectangle, and occasionally his full name as JOHN BURT, although there was no regulation or standard procedure. The place of manufacture was commonly added on early nineteenth-century silver from Philadelphia and New York, where craftsmen, influenced by the marks on imported English silver, also indulged in the use of pseudo hall-marks.

The quality of the metal followed the English standard of Sterling, in which 925 out of every 1,000 parts are pure silver, with the remaining 75 parts composed of copper as an alloy to harden the metal, or 11 ounces 10 pennyweight pure silver in every troy pound (12 ounces). Many a colonial silversmith warranted his wares "as good as Sterling" in contemporary newspaper advertisements. As early as 1753 the inhabitants of Philadelphia, in consequence of the "Yearly considerable Quantity of Silver and Gold wrought in This Province, not only for the Inhabitants, but also for several of the neighboring Provinces and West India Islands," petitioned the Provincial Council of Pennsylvania for the establishment of an assay office to regulate, assay and stamp gold and silver "wrought in this Province, agreeable to the Laws and Customs of Great Britain." The following year a supporting Bill was introduced into the General Assembly but failed to be enacted. It was introduced with amendments in 1756, 1767, 1769 and 1770, when it was voted down by a large majority. It was not until 1814 with the enactment of a law by the

Plate 1

The Intent of the Frontiſpiece.

1 *St.* Dunſtan, *the Patron of the* Goldſmiths *Company.*

2 *The Refining Furnace.*

3 *The* Teſt *with Silver refining on it.*

4 *The Fineing Bellows.*

5 *The Man blowing or working them.*

6 *The* Teſt *Mould.*

7 *A Wind-hole to melt Silver in without Bellows.*

8 *A pair of* Organ *Bellows.*

9 *A Man melting or Boiling, or nealing Silver at them.*

10 *A Block, with a large Anvil placed thereon.*

11 *Three Men Forging Plate.*

12 *The Fineing and other* Goldſmiths *Tools.*

13 *The* Aſſay *Furnace.*

14 *The* Aſſay*-Master making Aſſays.*

15 *His Man putting the Aſſays into the Fire.*

16 *The Warden marking the Plate on the Anvil.*

17 *His Officer holding the Plate for the Marks.*

18 *Three* Goldſmiths, *ſmall-workers, at work.*

19 *A* Goldſmiths *Shop furniſhed with Plate.*

20 *A* Goldſmith *weighing Plate.*

Frontispiece of A New Touchstone for Gold and Silver Wares by W.B., *London, 1679; the standard 17th-century reference book on metalwork. The forge, bellows, and tools are typical of those of the craft, of which St. Dunstan was the patron saint*

Plate 2

a) *Massachusetts coinage minted at Boston, 1652 to 1663 or later, by John Hull and Robert Sanderson.* Left to right: *New England shilling, willow shilling & sixpence, oaktree shilling & twopence, pine-tree shilling & sixpence*

b) *Development of the Spoon, 1650–1850.* Upper left (1) *slip-end* c. 1650; (2) *puritan* c. 1660; (3 & 4) *trifid* c. 1690; (5) *wavy-end* c. 1700; (6 & 7) *mid-rib* c. 1715; Lower left (1) *modified mid-rib* c. 1750; (2) *feather-edge* c. 1770; (3 & 4) *bright-cut* c. 1785; (5) *coffin-end* c. 1800; *fiddle-shell* c. 1830–50

General Assembly of Maryland that one finds state regulation. Under its terms Baltimore silver was required to contain 11 oz. fine silver in every troy pound, the old Scottish standard, and was subject to assay by the assay officer who stamped it with town mark, assay mark and date letter. Until modification of the law in 1830, this was the only silver stamped with legally required marks. The use of the word *Sterling* is not commonly found until after 1860, with the possible exception of Baltimore silver of the 1800-1814 period. Its equivalent term *Standard* is sometimes found on pieces dating from the 1830's. After 1850, the letters D, C and the terms COIN or PURE COIN are found on silver indicating the pieces to be fashioned from dollars or other silver coins. The U.S. Coin standard in the nineteenth century was 900 parts pure silver with 100 parts alloy, thus slightly lower than that of Sterling.

The Foster arms by Edward Winslow on the rim of a plate

Chapter Two

The Seventeenth Century

AMONG THE PASSENGERS OF THE "PHOENIX," SAILING TO VIRGINIA in 1608, were listed two goldsmiths, two refiners and a jeweller. That these men were not intended to practise their craft is confirmed by the statement of Captain John Smith that "the lust of gold was apparent in sending out refiners and goldsmiths, who never had occasion to exercise their craft; as also the jeweller for there were no precious stones nor jewels, save only such few pearls as might be found in the oysters, of which there are plenty." The gold for which these men were searching could not be found "for the best of reasons that there was none to find." The subsequent discovery and cultivation of tobacco and the springing-up of widely scattered plantations, whose owners had close contact with England, was not encouraging to the growth of the silversmith's trade; and it is likely that little plate, with the possible exception of a few spoons, was made in Virginia during the seventeenth century. What plate has survived the whims of fashion in the churches and plantation families of tidewater Virginia is of London make.

The chief centers of silversmithing activity in the period of settlement were the port towns of Boston and New York. Inasmuch as silver is such a personal thing and its production part and parcel of the life of the people, reflecting as it does the racial background, social, economic and political conditions of its day, one cannot disassociate it from its maker or its original owner. Boston, the largest and most important colonial port during the seventeenth century, was largely inhabited by English settlers who had come to establish permanent homes, some hoping to advance their social and economic standing, others seeking freedom from political troubles or religious persecution. Daniel Neal, in his *History of New England* (1720), estimated the value taken from England by 1640 to the four New England settlements at some £500,000, "but if the Persecution of the Puritans had continued 10 or 12 years longer, I am apt to think that a fourth part of the Riches of the Kingdom would have been carried out of it." Some of these settlers brought a considerable amount of their plate with them. The Rev. José Glover, non-conforming rector of Sutton in Surrey, suspended for refusing as a conscientious Puritan to read King Charles's *Book of Sports* from his pulpit, sailed with his family for America in 1638. The plate brought over by the Glovers, as revealed in subsequent estate litigation, is evidence of a much more polite way of living than is generally supposed, for it consisted of "29 siluer spones, a very faire salt with 3 full knops on the top of it, 3 other siluer salts of lesser sorts, a great siluer trunke with $\frac{4}{1}$ knop to sta[n]d on the table and with suger: 6 porrengers, one small one: 3 bere boules, 4 wine cupes, a siluer grate with a Couer on it: 6 siluer trencher plates." Of these the "faire salt" and possibly the small porringer are preserved in the collection of Harvard College plate. They are fashioned in the style current in the reign of Charles I.

William Harris's observation, made in Boston in 1675, that "The merchants seem to be rich men, and their houses as handsomely furnished as most in London" is borne out by the wills and inventories recorded in the Suffolk County Probate Court. In 1653 Capt. William Tyng's estate listed in its plate: "2 beare bowls, double gilt salt, 4 tankards, gilt can, caudle cupp, colker bowl [probably wood with silver mounts], 2 spoons, 4 porringers, 2 wine cupps, 1 bason, 2 dram cupps, great salt, 2 silver bottles, 2 trencher salts."

In 1669 Antipas Boyse had "a case with spoone, fork and knife, 1 tankard, 1 large salt cellar, 1 caudell cup, a porringer, 1 plate, 2 lilly pots with covers [covered cups], 1 cup, 1 dram cup, 12 newe spoones, 3 old, 1 small porringer, 9 buttons for breeches, thimble, trencher salt" weighing 161½ oz. which at 6 shillings per oz. was valued at £45 15s. 11d. In 1672 Governor Bellingham left 116 ounces of plate consisting of a caudle cup, 2 tankards, 2 salts, 3 beare cups, 1 wine cup, 1 dram cup, 1 porringer, sugar dish, and 10 spoons valued at £34 16s. The rich merchant Capt. John Freake who was killed by an explosion in Boston Harbor in 1675 left "2 siluer tankards, 2 Inckhornes, 1 sault seller, 1 sugar box, 1 caudle cup with cover, 1 cup with cover, 1 plate, 1 candlestick, 1 bason, 6 porringers, 3 wine cupps, a graiter case and cheese toaster, 24 spoones, 8 forkes" valued at £68 along with "a whissle silver chaine and childe's bell" at 15 shillings and "his own Signet and Sett of Gould Buttons . . . £3." The richness of his plate is in keeping with his portrait painted at Boston in 1674, showing an arrogant man of fashion garbed in a suit enriched with silver buttons and an elaborate collar of Venetian lace and wearing on his little finger his gold signet ring.

The Royal Governor, Sir William Phipps, first New Englander to be knighted, left in 1696 a total of 1,240 oz. of unitemized plate which must have been particularly fine since it was appraised at the rate of 6s. 8d. per oz., an advance of 8d. per oz. In 1697 the inventory of Hezekiah Usher, Jr., lists 2 tankards, 1 sillibub pot and cover, 2 salts, 1 mustard pot and spoon, 1 plate, 5 trencher salts, 1 wine cup and cover for a goblet, 1 chafing dish and bottom weighing 157½ oz. valued at £53 3s. and a notation of "186½ oz. of plate in Mr. Brattle's hands" valued at £62 18s. 10d.

The prosperity suggested by these inventories was partly responsible for the establishment of a mint at Boston in 1652 by the General Court of Massachusetts. Coinage was the prerogative of the Crown but Charles I had been executed not long before and Charles II had been proclaimed King only in the colonies of Virginia and Maryland. The Court appointed, as mint master, twenty-eight-year-old John Hull, who had learned the art of silversmithing from his elder half-brother, London-trained Richard Storer. Hull records in his Diary, 1652:

> Also upon occasion of much counterfeit coin brought in the country, and much loss accruing in that respect (and that did occasion a stoppage of trade), the General Court

ordered a mint to be set up, and to coin it, bringing it to the sterling standard for fineness, and for weight every shilling to be three pennyweight, i.e., 9d. at 5s. per oz. and they made choice of me for that employment; and I chose my friend, Robert Sanderson, to be my partner to which the Court consented.

Although the New England coin maintained the English standard the English shilling weighed 4 pennyweight, Hull's only 3. That it was meant for circulation only in New England is indicated by the General Court's order forbidding exportation of more than 20 shillings; the penalty for violation was forfeiture of the culprit's whole estate, one-third to go to the informer.

The first coins issued were circular with N.E. stamped on the obverse, and on the reverse the value, in Roman numerals, for shillings, sixpence and three-penny bits. A few months later, to prevent counterfeiting and clipping by the unscrupulous, the General Court decreed the addition of a double ring on each side of the coin, with the legend *Massachusetts* enclosing a tree on one side and *New England, Anno Domini* surrounding the value of the piece and the date on the other. The first "tree issue" coin was decorated with a crudely executed willow. In 1662 this was replaced with a new pattern featuring an oak with the addition of a two-pence piece dated 1662, the other denominations retaining the 1652 date. In 1663, the pine tree was adopted and was issued in the three larger denominations, all dated 1652, until the mint was abolished in 1688 (Plate 2a). Hull, who received one out of every twenty shillings coined, became one of Boston's wealthiest merchants and the tradition of his wealth and his plump, only daughter supplied Nathaniel Hawthorne with one of his most charming legends, "The Grandfather's Chair."

Many of these Bay shillings, as they were currently known, found their way back to the shop of John Hull (1624–1683) and his partner, London-trained Robert Sanderson (1608–1693). The latter probably did most of the actual work, judging from the reference by Hull's son-in-law, Samuel Sewall, to "Mr. Saunderson and all that wrought in the Shop under him." The earliest pieces which have survived fires, wars and the melting pot are based on the styles of Charles I; although examples of Jacobean plate have been preserved in the collections of church silver, there was no attempt to copy them, judging from surviving pieces. The commonest object was the spoon and the earliest form has a deep fig-shaped bowl and a slender polygonal handle, whose end, sliced off at an oblique angle resembling a slipped stalk, accounts for the name "slip-end" spoon. Two examples by Hull and Sanderson (Plate 2b), as well as one by their apprentice, Jeremiah Dummer (1645–1718), have survived. This style, popular in England during the Commonwealth, dates back to the fifteenth century. The natural successor to the slip-end spoon was the "Puritan" spoon whose handle was a flattened strip with a shallower bowl of a rounded oval shape—a style popular in England during the Commonwealth. Only three examples, one each by Hull and Sanderson, Jeremiah Dummer, and his brother-in-law, John Coney (1656–1722), are known to have survived.

Following the restoration of Charles II, a continental spoon with a flat handle split at the end into three parts and known as "trifid," was introduced into England and became popular in Boston by 1690. The oval bowl was ornamented on the back with a ridged tongue sometimes surrounded by elaborate leafy scrolls struck in slight relief from a swage. This form of ornament was occasionally repeated on the front of the handle (Plate 2b). These spoons were more or less of a uniform size, a little smaller than the tablespoon of today. Although forks are mentioned in the inventories quoted above, the only surviving specimens are sucket forks, a combination spoon and fork used for sweetmeats, wet or dry, a favorite seventeenth-century dessert. One pair that still survives was fashioned before 1689 by William Rouse (1639–1705), the enterprising silversmith with whom Jasper Danckers lodged during his visit to Boston in 1680. Danckers in his Journal refers to Rouse's activity in connection with a trip to Roxbury to see John Eliot, the famous "Apostle to the Indians," a trip on which "Our landlord had promised to take us; but was not able to do so, in consequence of his having too much business."

Of great popularity was the porringer. The earliest example by Hull and Sanderson (Page 9) is a straight-sided bowl of pint capacity with a single, flat, pierced handle of simple design. By 1695 this type of bowl had become curved with an everted rim and the handle pierced in an elaborate geometric pattern of circles, quatrefoils, cinquefoils, hearts and crescents (Page 24). These handles were cast, and it is likely, from the similarity of surviving examples, that the silversmiths borrowed or pirated fellow craftsmen's patterns. All New England handle patterns are based on English styles with the exception of one used by the Huguenot craftsman, Capt. René Grignon (Page 11), recalling one on a Brest écuelle of 1681 (Collection of the Marquis de Langle). A similar handle has been noted on two porringers by Jeremiah Dummer.

The beaker served both secular and ecclesiastical purposes and was of two types. One type had a straight body with flat bottom and was decorated with such a broad granulated band as that on the beaker fashioned in 1659 by Hull and Sanderson for the First Church, Boston—in whose possession it still remains. The other type has a flaring lip with a plain moulded base; numerous examples by Hull and Sanderson, Dummer, Coney and Rouse have survived.

Popular as a communion vessel was the standing wine cup of the time of Charles I. One of these tall cups on a slender baluster stem made in London 1626–7 was brought to New England by an early immigrant, Atherton Hough, Mayor of Boston, Lincolnshire, and was bequeathed by him to the First Church of Boston, Massachusetts, where it is still in use. This style was succeeded by cups of wine-glass shape with larger bowls, shorter and thicker baluster stems. An example made in London in 1639–40 (distinguished by its matted decoration) and bequeathed to the First Church of Boston, served as a model for one made by Hull and Sanderson for the same church, where both were members. A plainer example (Plate 3a) was fashioned by them in 1674 for the Church of Rehoboth, Plymouth Colony, from a £5 legacy of Capt. Thomas Willett, who was the first English-speaking Mayor of New York (Mabel Brady Garvan Collection, Yale University). Its simplicity of line and complete lack of decoration are most appropriate to its function. One feels that it has much in common with such stark portraits of New England divines as the one of John Davenport painted at Boston in 1670, and now in the collection of Yale University.

The most popular drinking vessel, judging from the inventories in an age "potent in potting," was the cider or ale tankard, with its straight tapering body re-enforced by a moulded base and rim, a low flat cover, raised by a horizontal ram's horn or cupped thumbpiece, and a massive scroll handle terminating in a shield. There is a widespread misconception that the vents or holes at the end of the tankard handle were constructed for use as "whistles" to summon the tap-boy to replenish the drained vessel. These holes were in fact intended as inlets of cold air during the process of construction. Without them the air in the hollow handle, which is composed of two hammered strips soldered together, would expand when heated for soldering, and on contracting during cooling would result in a misshapen surface. One might add that these vents appear on the handles of church flagons as well. All surviving examples by Sanderson, Dummer, Coney, and Rouse follow the general form.

More elaborate and closer to current English fashions is a tankard by Timothy Dwight (1654–1691/2) which has a surbase decorated with a border of repoussé and chased acanthus leaves and a sejant lion for a thumbpiece, features popular in English silver of the Charles II period. The usual capacity was a quart but two larger examples (Plate 3b) are known, one by Jeremiah Dummer, the other by his master, Robert Sanderson, fashioned for Isaac and Mary Vergoose (Museum of Fine Arts, Boston). Isaac's second wife, Elizabeth, who inherited the tankard, was the original baby-sitter and the songs with which she lulled the Boston babes became the inspiration for *Mother Goose Rhymes* traditionally published by her son-in-law, Thomas Fleet.

Vying with the tankard for popularity was the gourd-shaped cup with two cast scrolled handles, often decorated with caryatid thumb grips, with or without covers. It was used to serve caudle, a warm drink consisting of thin gruel mixed with wine or ale, sweetened and spiced. No proper baptism, wedding, feast or funeral was complete without its caudle.

Other popular drinks served from these cups were posset, made of hot milk curdled with wine, ale or other beverage and flavored with sugar and spices, and syllabub, made of milk or cream, curdled by the admixture of wine or cider, sweetened and flavored. Many of the early cups are plain, some decorated with punched work or flat-chased tulips against a matted ground, reminiscent of the carved ornament on the chests and

Plate 3

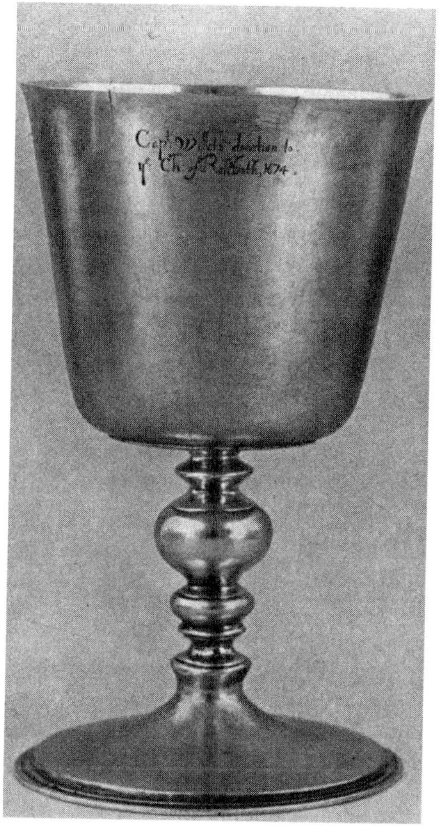

a) *Standing cup of 1674 by Hull and Sanderson, purchased from a legacy of £5. Height $7\frac{1}{4}$"*

b) *An excellent example of balance between design and hammerwork is demonstrated in this capacious cider tankard by Hull's London-trained partner, Robert Sanderson. Height $8\frac{3}{16}$"*

Plate 4

a) *The quality of the cast caryatid handles, together with the vigorous simple lines of this covered caudle cup of 1679, attest to John Coney's expert craftsmanship. One of the earliest surviving examples of American heraldic engraving on silver is shown in the Addington arms. Height* $6\frac{7}{8}$"

b) *Coney's ability with the graver is ably demonstrated in this detail of the richly engraved border on a 17th-century plate. Diameter* $11\frac{3}{16}$"

cupboards of the Connecticut River Valley. Many a caudle cup has survived today as a result of having been willed by its owner to the church as a communion vessel. The large plain covered one (Plate 4a), with finely cast caryatid handles (Garvan Collection), by John Coney fashioned in 1679 is unique and strongly resembles the popular contemporary Venetian glass forms. The influence of the more florid English style is reflected by 1690 in the charming cup by Coney in which the lower part of the body is modelled in low relief with a gay embossed band of roses, pinks, and cherubs (Plate 8b). It was the inspiration of Oliver Wendell Holmes' delightful poem "On Lending a Punch Bowl," and is now owned by the poet's great-nephew. Another by Coney, identical in form and decoration, is among the Harvard College collection of silver.

A type of drinking vessel largely confined to this century was the dram cup. Its small shallow bowl with flat or twisted wire handles suited for a short dram, the seventeenth century's generic term for distilled spirits, a welcome drink in the chill New England houses. Despite their small size, numerous examples by Hull and Sanderson, Benjamin Sanderson, Dummer, Coney, and Edward Winslow have survived from an era in which innkeepers were warned to "suffer none to be drunk, or to have above half a pint of wine, or to sit above half an Hour, or after Nine at Night."

By 1685, John Dutton, author of *Letters from New England*, states that "the beverage most esteemed by everyone was a bowl of punch," an Indian drink made of lemon water and Madeira or brandy. The earliest bowl, fashioned in 1692 by Jeremiah Dummer, has straight sides decorated with flat-chased conventional floral sprays recalling Stuart embroidery patterns, curving to a flat bottom with the brim scalloped in the Portuguese manner. The finely cast handles have snakehead terminals (Plate 5) (Garvan Collection). It is likely that the large caudle cups also served as punch bowls in an age that was strictly utilitarian.

Among the new pieces introduced into New England was the salver which in Thomas Blount's *Glossographia* (1661) is described as "a new fashioned piece of wrought plate, broad and flat, with a foot underneath, and is used in giving Beer or other liquid thing to save the Carpit or

Cloathes from drops." The only surviving example is one by Timothy Dwight in the Pickman Collection. On its broad rim are engraved floral sprays and wild beasts of Oriental inspiration. Perhaps the flat plate by Coney in the same collection served a similar purpose. With its broad rim beautifully engraved with a repeating pattern of cherub's heads, tulips and carnations, it is one of the most delightful pieces of American silver (detail Plate 4b).

In the absence of forks and knives, table etiquette demanded the use of the rosewater basin, a broad-rimmed shallow bowl with domed center which still graces the feasts of the London City Companies, and which was, between courses, passed with a napkin to the guests. Two such vessels have survived as baptismal basins in New England churches. One fashioned by Coney was bequeathed by its owner Dame Mary Saltonstall, relict of the Governor of Connecticut, to the Old South Church, Boston; the other was the gift of his Harvard students to tutor William Brattle and is inscribed on the rim: *Ex dono Pupillorum, 1695*. The recipient was in the following year ordained pastor of the Church of Christ, Cambridge, and in his will in 1716 occurs the clause: "I bequeath and present to the Church of Christ in Cambridge for a baptismal basin, my great silver basin, an inscription upon which I leave to the prudence of the Rev'd President and the R^d. Mr. Simon Bradstreet." The "prudent" inscription reads:

A Baptismall Basin consecrated, bequeathd & presented to the Church of Christ in Cambridge, his Dearly beloved Flock, by the Rev^d. M^r. W^m. Brattle Past^r. of the S^d. Church: Who was translated from his charge to his Crown, Feb^r. 15: 1716/17. [First Church, Unitarian, Cambridge.]

Unfortunately no salt, sugar box, chafing dish or mustard pot made in seventeenth-century New England has survived the changes in fashion. Among the pieces that attest to their craftsman's skill is a noble pair of hammered square-sectioned candlesticks made prior to 1686 by Jeremiah Dummer. The shafts simulating clustered columns banded together in the Gothic fashion rest on a square wide-spreading moulded foot (Plate 6a). In form the design closely resembles the mediaeval clustered chimney of seventeenth-century New England architecture.

Plate 5

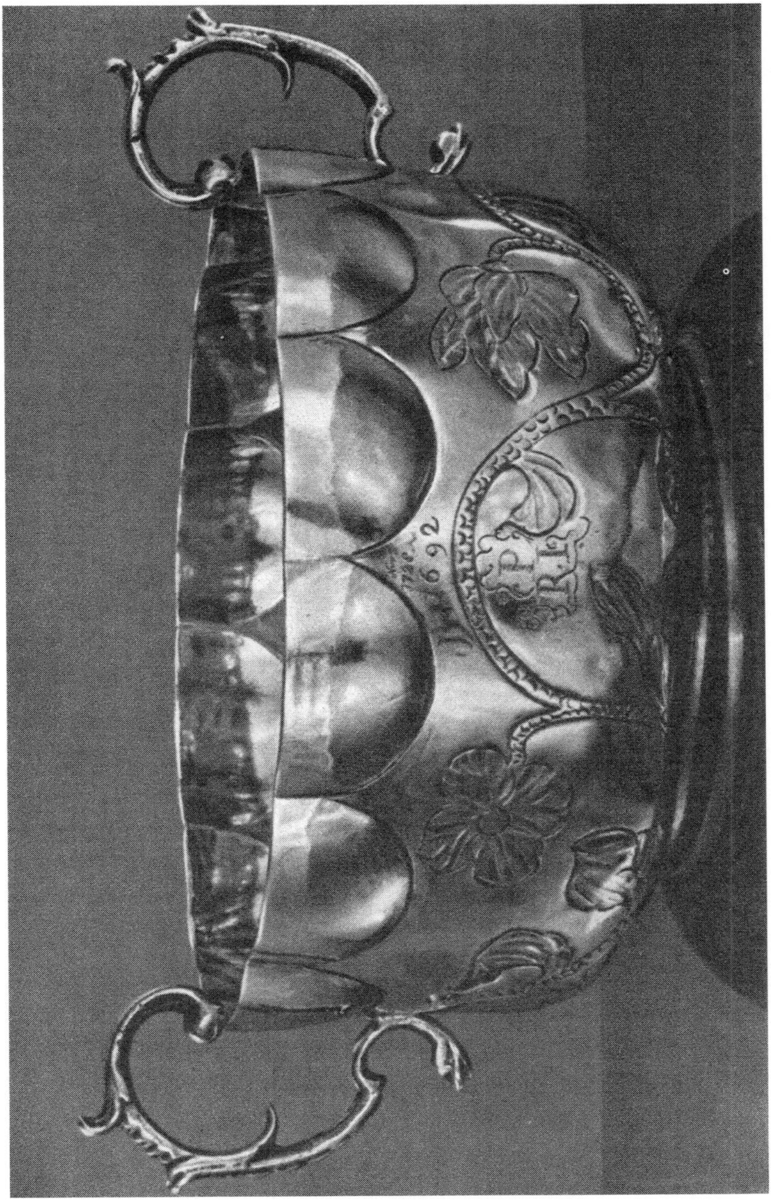

Dummer's punch bowl of 1692 shows a combination of Portuguese form with English decoration of stiff floral pattern in flat chasing, reminiscent of Stuart embroidery. Diameter 6¾"

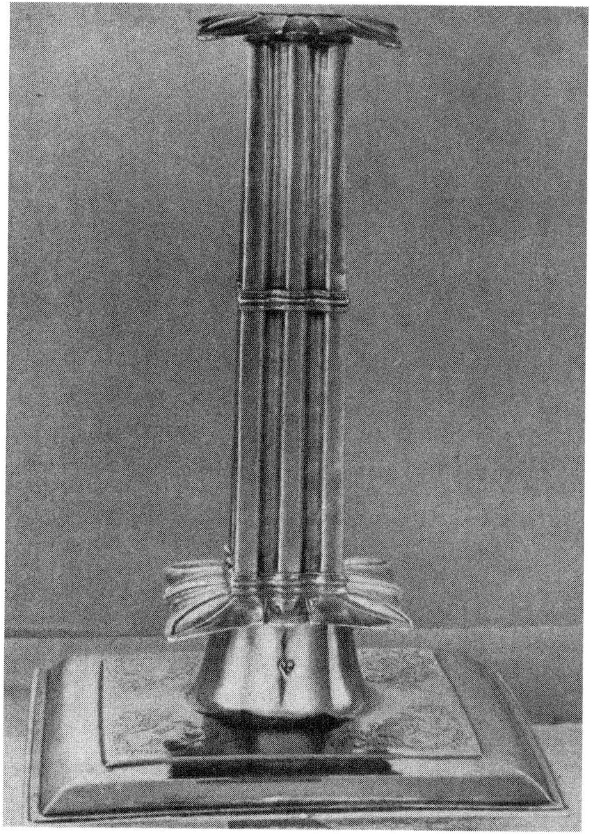

a) *Dummer's candlestick of 1686 simulates in its clustered column the central pilastered chimney found in 17th-century New England architecture. Height 10¾"*

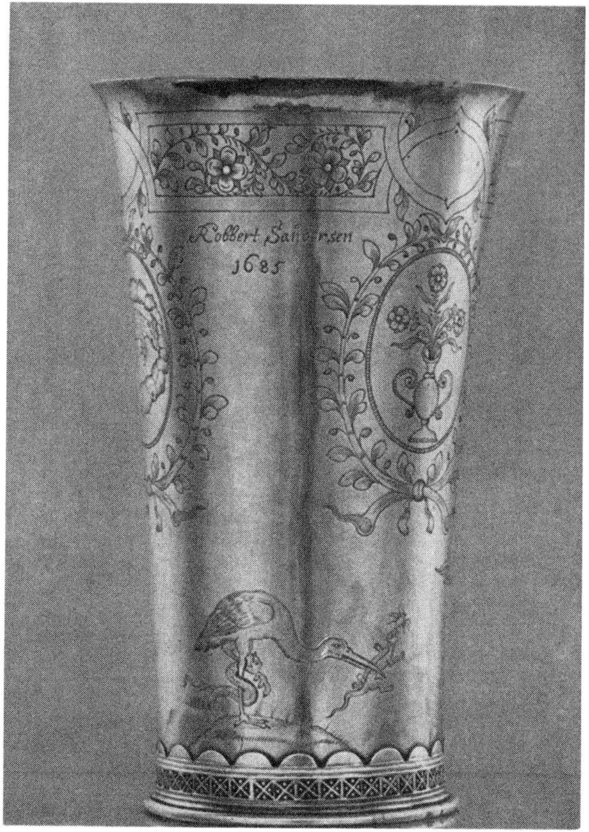

b) *Characteristic of the Dutch heritage in form and ornament is Cornelis van der Burch's 1685 beaker. The engraved emblems are from the illustrations to the didactic poems of Jacobus Cats. Height 8"*

What a touch of colour this plate must have made when spread upon the velvet cloth of the court or press cupboard in the low-ceilinged parlor. And although the forms are for the most part based on English styles, there is by 1690 a noticeable difference in the pieces produced here. In its quality of sturdiness, reflecting the living conditions under which it was produced and the type of life for which it was made, the silver had acquired the same American flavor and individuality that distinguished it from English silver, just as the New Englander differed from the old Englander.

New York, or New Amsterdam, as it was known until ceded to England, was inhabited largely by Dutch settlers, whose possessions, brought over from Holland, reflected their cultural heritage, a heritage to which their descendants clung tenaciously. For although New Amsterdam finally passed under English rule by the Treaty of Westminster in 1674, Dutch settlers and their descendants continued trade with Holland and spoke the Dutch tongue in church and market until well past the middle of the eighteenth century. The great period of New York's prosperity dates from the period of English administration and was based largely upon the flourishing fur trade as well as the flour and bread monopoly enjoyed by the city, from 1678 to 1694, and memorialized in the beavers, flour barrels and windmill sails of the city's coat-of-arms.

A new and far greater source of wealth flowed in through the pirate trade; in fact by 1698 it had grown so flagrant that the Earl of Bellomont was sent over as Governor with strict orders to suppress it. In his reports to the London Board of Trade, Bellomont confirmed what had been for a long time suspected, namely, that "This city hath been a nest of Pirates, and I already find that several of their ships have their owners and were fitted from this Port . . . Two men in this town had for their share £12,000 each, which were brought from Madagascar and got there with the barter with pirates. Besides there came home to the mouth of this port 8 or 9 pirate ships since my coming to this government, which would have brought in a vast quantity of those goods, and by the confession of the merchants in the town they would have brought in a £100,000 in gold and silver."

This indulgence by the staid New York burghers in such a trade together with the inherent Dutch love of substantial possessions encouraged patronage of the silversmith, as evidenced in their early wills and inventories. In 1682, Asser Levy, a butcher, had 22 spoons, 1 fork, 4 goblets, a tankard, a mustard pot, cup with two ears, 4 small cups, 2 salt cellars, 2 cups, 2 saucers, a spice box, tumbler, bell "one Cornelia tree cup and two dishes with silver"; four years later Mayor Cornelius Steenwyck left 723 ounces of unitemized plate, valued at £216 18s.; the widow Sarah Oort, prior to her marriage to William Kidd in 1690, inherited 164 oz. of silver worth £101 9s., including a tankard, cup, plate, sugar box and spoon, salt cellar, 2 porringers, a tumbler and 12 spoons; William Pleay owned "a jocolato pot" (1690); Lewis Morris in 1692 left 900 ounces of unitemized plate.

In her will, proved in 1693, Christina Cappoens, a widow, made the following bequests: to her daughter Maria a silver beaker, one gold rose diamond ring, a silver cup, pepper box, silver cup with a silver cover and 3 silver spoons; to grand-daughter Sara Molenaer, a salt-cellar marked with the full name of Christina Roselaers and marked with her coat-of-arms, a silver beaker marked the same, and a silver mustard pot marked with the name of Jacob Hay, a church book with silver clasps and chain, a silver cup, 6 silver spoons, silver chain, one great ear-spangle with ear jewels and largest hoop ring, a gold finger ring with a diamond in it and a tumbler marked J. H.; to Catrina Praa, a silver beaker and 6 silver spoons marked J. H. According to the appraisal by Jacobus van der Spiegel, the silver beaker weighing 12 oz. at 7s. made £4 4s.; the gold rose diamond ring, £5; the pepper box, 2¼ oz. at 7s., 17s. 6d.; the beaker marked "Christina Roselaers," 16 oz. at 7s., £5 12s.; the salt, 14 oz., £4 10s.; one Church book with silver clasps and chain £1 16s.; the gold ear pendant and jewels weighing "2 oz. good," at £5 per ounce, £10.

The characteristic early New York spoon differs from that of New England in that it is made in two parts, a hammered round bowl to which is attached a cast handle whose terminus varies from a hind's hoof to an owl sejant or caryatid figure with leafy scrolls based on Dutch models. They were often used at funerals as a *memento mori* for the chief mourners. By 1690 the trifid handle had made its appearance but in a somewhat broader form than the New England type. The sucket fork was also popular as evidenced by inventories and the surviving pairs by Jesse Kip and Bartholomew LeRoux.

The most characteristically Dutch object was the beaker, which is found in both secular and ecclesiastical use, the only difference being in the subject-matter of the engraved ornament. With wide flaring lip, re-enforced at the base with an applied band of stamped design or leaf ornament, they follow closely the Dutch beakers imported from Holland. The lip is richly engraved with a broad double interlacing band enclosing a conventional pattern of flowers and leaves from which depend floral sprays. Church beakers are usually engraved with vignettes enclosing figures symbolic of Faith, Hope and Charity. Such a beaker, fashioned at Haarlem in 1660, was presented to the First Reformed Church, Albany, where in 1678 it served as a model for one made by Ahasuerus Hendricks, an early silversmith of New York. Another with similar decoration was fashioned by an unidentified I B, probably Jeurian Blanck, Jr., in 1683 for the Reformed Church at Kingston (Clearwater Collection, Metropolitan Museum of Art). An almost identical beaker by the same maker, dated 1684, is still in the collection of the First Reformed Protestant Church of Brooklyn. A pair with a slightly different pattern of ornament were fashioned by Gerrit Onckelbag (1670–1733) in 1697 for the Flatbush Reformed Church. The finest surviving secular example is the imposing presentation beaker (Plate 6b), a traditional gift to Robert Sanders for his successful efforts as intermediator in a real-estate transaction between Robert Livingston, Lord of the Manor, and the Mohawk Indians, made in 1685 by Cornelis van der Burch (1653–1699), New York's first native-born silversmith (Garvan Collection). The source of five of the six designs enriching its surface have been traced to Adriaen van der Venne's engravings illustrating the didactic poems of Jacobus Cats, favorite leisure reading in Knickerbocker New York.

By far the most popular vessel in New York and one of the most individualistic was the tankard, which illustrates the result of the impact of two cultures. Completely unlike the few surviving Holland tankards, it is basically the English form with certain characteristics adapted from Dutch or Scandinavian sources. Prominent among these characteristics are the inset medal or coin on the cover, the rich applied cast or chased ornament on the handle and tip, the horizontal elongated spiral of the corkscrew thumbpiece, and the band of acanthus leaf with meandering wire applied above the base moulding, as on beakers. On the whole, the New York tankard is larger and heavier than its Boston contemporary. A tankard by Gerrit Onckelbag in the Clearwater Collection has engraved upon its cover a representation of the *Nassau*, a ship engaged in pirate trade, and according to tradition was presented, as an expression of gratitude by the stockholders in the highly profitable venture, to that Capt. Giles Shelly who in the words of Lord Bellomont "lately come from Madagascar with 50 or 60 pirates has so flushed them at New York with Arabian gold and East India goods."

The mug in pint and quart size followed the same general lines as the tankard but had no cover. Another drinking vessel was the tumbler, a small straight-sided bowl with rounded bottom used for wine and dram.

Three two-handled cups have survived from the last decade of the century. The body of each, slightly rounded at the base, is richly decorated with a surbase of repoussé and chased acanthus leaves and rests on a low moulded base. The two cast eared-handles are suggestive of the caryatid type. The slightly domed cover is decorated in relief with a central rose bordered with leafy scrolls against a matted ground. Applied equidistantly are three shaped brackets which serve the double purpose of handles or feet on which the cover may rest in an inverted position as a saucer or stand for the cup. One of these (Plate 7), fashioned in 1696 by Gerrit Onckelbag, was a godmother's gift to her grand-daughter, who was baptized a week after the Dutch children's gift-giving festival of St. Nicholas (Garvan Collection).

The influx of French silversmiths in the 1680's may be partly responsible for the high quality of craftsmanship which marks the work of the late seventeenth and early eighteenth centuries. In 1685 Louis XIV's Revocation of the Edict of Nantes had driven the Protestants from France. In 1687 his decree calling for the melting of all plate and forbidding

Plate 7

Another instance of the combination of an English form with rich Dutch ornament is to be found in the covered caudle cup by Gerrit Onckelbag, decorated with repoussé and flat-chased ornament. Typical of Dutch New York heraldic engraving is the rendering of the Bayard arms. Height $5\frac{3}{4}$"

a) *The opulent, boldly executed ornament of Bartholomew LeRoux's punch bowl is typical of 17th-century New York silver. Note the finely cast caryatid handles. Diameter 9"*

b) *The playful treatment of the embossed decoration of Coney's caudle cup indicates the influence of Stuart England in Puritan New England by 1690. Height 5½"*

any further manufacture forced many of the remaining silversmiths to seek their livelihood in a new land. Many came to the colonies, and by 1690 it was estimated that one-tenth of New York City's population was French. Strangely enough these craftsmen, many of whom had come via Holland, introduced little of their native styles other than the cut-card ornament, but quickly adapted themselves to the taste and demands of their new home. The outstanding Huguenot craftsman in New York was Bartholomew Le Roux (1663–1713), maker of two massive two-handled punch bowls of pumpkin shape, divided into panels richly decorated with repoussé and chased patterns of tulips, roses and other floral forms so dear to the heart of the Dutch (Plate 8a). A simpler bowl by the same maker was fashioned for a Quaker client of New Jersey and has in its plain panels a flat-chased fleur-de-lys near the foot (Garvan Collection). Bowls of this shape, at least six of which have survived, appear to have been made only in New York, and basically they are unlike any Dutch prototype with which they have previously been compared.

Although two richly ornamented standing salts of Holland make have been handed down in an Albany family, no American example is known to have survived. A trencher salt, octagonal in form, by Cornelis van der Burch is still preserved by descendants of Jacobus and Eva van Cortlandt, for whom it was made in 1691.

Two baptismal basins are still preserved in the churches for which they were made. One at Tarrytown is the work of an unidentified I B; the other in the South Reformed Church in New York has inscribed on its wide flat rim a poetical effusion in Low Dutch composed by the minister, Dominie Selyns, explaining the inner meaning of baptism. It was made in 1694 by Jacobus van der Spiegel (1668–1708) at a cost of 63 Holland guilders.

Of the other seaport towns established during the century, Philadelphia and Charleston had their own craftsmen, while Newport seems to have been supplied by Boston shops, judging from the archives and the few surviving pieces. Two Huguenot silversmiths are recorded at Charleston, Nicolas de Longuemare, Jr., who arrived in 1686 following the

Revocation of the Edict of Nantes, and whose account books are preserved, and Solomon Legaré, but unfortunately none of their works has survived the changing fashions and the ravages of war.

Philadelphia being the last of the settlements to be established was probably the most advanced stylistically, if the surviving architecture is any criterion. That silversmiths were well established before the end of the century is evident from Gabriel Thomas's glowing account of the city, published in 1698, in which he states that "Silversmiths . . . have between Half a Crown and Three Shillings an Ounce for working their Silver and for Gold equivalent." César Ghiselin, Charles Pickering, William Paschall and Johannis Nys are known to have been working in Philadelphia prior to 1700 and yet possibly only one piece, a trifid spoon by Nys, can be attributed to these early days (Collection of Mr. and Mrs. Walter M. Jeffords).

One of the most interesting features of the silversmith's art lies in the engraved monograms, cyphers, inscriptions, ornament and heraldic devices. The earliest initials were placed in a triangular pattern with the initial of surname over the given initials of husband and wife. The earliest are often "pricked" and are reminiscent of contemporary ornament on New England bible boxes. By 1680, it was usual to engrave or cut the initial into the metal. Cyphers or double monograms were extremely popular in New York and decorated the fronts of tankards enclosed in feather plumes as, for example, on the one fashioned for Augustus Jay by Cornelis van der Burch; they also served as frequent decorations on the flat tankard covers, encircled with such richly engraved floral scrolls as on the pieces by Benjamin Wynkoop and Jacobus van der Spiegel.

The marking of plate with coats-of-arms associated with a family may be traced in England and on the continent to mediaeval times. References to their use in the colonies occur in early journals and wills. Such a use on plate is described by William Jefferey in his journal under the date of July 14, 1673:

Mistress Vaughan, the grandmother of the bridegroom, came . . . She giveth but one present at the marriage of each grandchild, always a silver cup, to be for the first born great-grandchild. She hath had inscribed on one side of this, the Latham arms, and desiring mine

Plate 9

The delightful counterpoise of plain and decorated surface is ably shown by Dummer's standing cup of 1701 in which the curved line of the cup is accentuated by alternating gadrooned and fluted ornament. Height 8 $\frac{11}{16}$"

Plate 10

a) *The last survival of a medieval tradition is to be found in the popular standing salt by Dummer with its gadrooned ornament characteristic of the William and Mary period. The scrolled brackets were for the support of a dish. Height* $5\frac{1}{2}''$

c) *The egg-shaped mustard pot with gadrooned foot by Peter van Dyck is the earliest known American exan and is based upon a Dutch model. Height* $5\frac{1}{4}''$

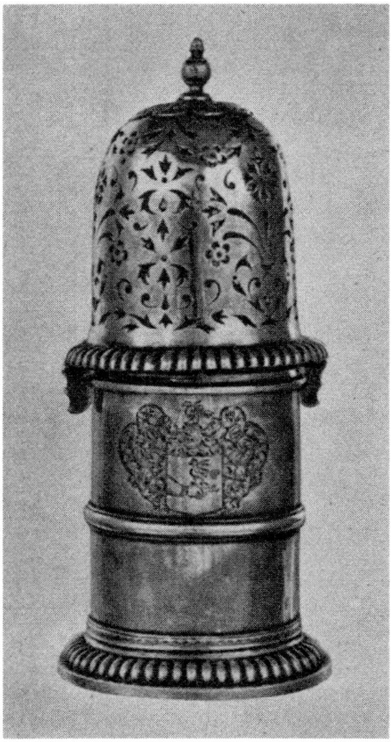

b) *The tall sugar caster engraved with the Schuyler arms by Peter van Dyck shows an early type of "bayonet" fastening and finely designed cover, boldly pierced in a floral pattern. Such a caster was one of a set of three, the other two for spices being somewhat smaller. Height* $7\frac{3}{4}''$

own on the other, as now joined in this marriage, it hath been done. Both families have long borne arms, regularly come by in ancient times, though some others do now claim arms on slight ground if report be true, having no warrant therefor.

The source of these arms is to be found in the seals and signet rings of the early settlers and in Guillim's *Display of Heraldry*, the standard English book on the subject.

The earliest designs in Boston follow the current English fashion, in which the device is displayed or "blazoned" on a straight-topped shield, except in the case of widows or spinsters, whose arms, in conformity with heraldic tradition, must be blazoned on a lozenge. The shield or lozenge is emphasized by enclosed decorative crossed plumes, a style popular in the reign of Charles II. Examples of heraldic engraving in this style are to be found in the Everard arms by Dummer on a pair of candlesticks, *c.* 1686, and in the Clarke arms by Coney on the baptismal basin of the Old South Church, Boston. A more conventional treatment was a blazoned shield topped by a closed helmet in profile on which rested the torse and crest, with an elaborate leafy mantling surrounding the shield on three sides, serving as its background—as in the Addington arms by Coney on the covered caudle cup of 1679 (Plate 4a) in the Garvan Collection. After 1690, the sides of the shield became shaped and the leafy mantling more profuse with full rounded curves, as in Coney's treatment of the Shrimpton arms on a 1692 tankard in the same collection. The treatment of the mantling in New York, based on Continental styles, shows a much bolder baroque pattern, as in the Bayard arms engraved by Onckelbag on a covered cup, *c.* 1696 (Garvan Collection). A characteristic Dutch New York feature is the use below the shield of pendent fruits, prominent among them being the pomegranate, a fertility symbol, which also appears on the contemporary New York kas or wardrobe. An excellent example occurs in Onckelbag's engraving of the Shelly arms on a tankard, *c.* 1698 (Clearwater Collection, Metropolitan Museum of Art). The proficiency of the silversmith-engraver in these early times not only enhances the beauty of these pieces but often offers a clue to rich associations with people and events long since forgotten.

CONEY

Chapter three

The Baroque of the William & Mary Style, 1700-1715

IN ENGLAND, FOLLOWING THE RESTORATION OF THE MONARCHY, there arose a tremendous demand for plate to replenish the collections of the great city companies, the colleges at Oxford and Cambridge, and the buffets of the gentry and rich merchants, most of which had been melted down during the Civil War. The introduction of luxuries by the court, as well as the general reaction against the restraints of the Commonwealth and puritanical aversion to beauty, prompted the use of bold design which by the time of the death of Charles II was chiefly expressed in gadrooned and fluted borders and surbases on vessels. So general was this demand and so profuse the work, that statutes had to be enacted to prevent a shortage of coin as a result of the wholesale melting.

While this fashion was at its height in England, New England was suffering from a long series of Indian attacks that inflicted great loss of life, property and trade. Daniel Neal writes that in 1699 "after a long and expensive War, the Affairs of the Country were settled on a solid Basis, Trade began to flourish and the People rejoyced in the Blessings of Peace." Imported clothes of the latest London fashion, and the arrival of a Royal Governor with the latest London plate, helped to stimulate the first generation of American-born New Englanders to offset their provincialism by acquiring things in the latest mode. This feeling is expressed in architecture, where the baroque forms of Sir Christopher Wren replaced the mediaeval characteristics of the seventeenth-century house. The angular, joined oaken furniture of the previous generation was discarded for the cabinet-maker's richly patterned walnut panels outlined by herring-bone bandings of the same wood. This contrasting surface richness was achieved by the silversmith through a counterpoise of plain and richly ornamented surfaces, in which the curved part of the body was accentuated by the use of gadrooned or fluted ornament. The earliest example known to the writer is a standing cup for communion made by Jeremiah Dummer in 1700. The bell-shaped cup, ornamented on the lower part of its body with alternating spiral gadrooning and fluting, rests on a baluster stem whose broad foot is enriched with a gadrooned band. That it must have been an early attempt by Dummer in this field of ornament is suggested by its timid treatment in contrast to three (Plate 9) executed by him in 1701, in which the boldly executed spirally gadrooned lines are repeated rhythmically, giving a delightful surface variation. This particular form, apparently a specialty with Dummer, was made solely for the New England churches.

Among the newly introduced ecclesiastical forms may be mentioned the tall plain flagon and simple chalice with paten cover, forming a part of the communion services presented to the Episcopal Churches of Boston, New York and Philadelphia by King William and Queen Mary. These undoubtedly were the models for those made by the American silversmiths.

The introduction of a more genteel form of living, with special rooms set aside for entertaining and dining, suggests a more elaborate service of plate, although function still played a large part in the life of the utilitarian New Englander.

The trifid spoon, which had continued to be popular in the early years of the period, was replaced by a modified form known today as "wavy-end" or "shield-top" from the shape of the handle, whose oval bowl had a plain rat-tail (Plate 2b). These are found in three sizes, table, porringer (a modified dessertspoon size) and teaspoon, the latter the size of the modern after-dinner coffee spoon. This style was also adopted in New

York and one of the finest examples (Plate III), fashioned in gold by Jacobus van der Spiegel (1668–1708), has in addition a pair of suspended bells, having been a christening gift in the de Peyster family (Garvan Collection). The seventeenth-century Dutch-type spoon with cast caryatid handles persisted well into this period; the largest single group is to be found in the Garvan Collection.

Porringers with spacious geometrically patterned handles are to be found in Boston and Philadelphia (Page 48). Their popularity is first evidenced in New York in this period, but as in the case of punch bowl and tankard, the handle receives a special and individualistic treatment. The intricate geometric design features a cross, heart and diamond and surviving examples by Peter van Dyck, Jacobus van der Spiegel, Bartholomew Schaats and Peter van Inburgh with slight variations, due probably to the mould, all follow the general pattern, which is confined to this locality (Page 8). Occasionally porringers are found with covers, and an unusual covered two-handled example in the manner of a French écuelle by Jan Nieuwkirk is in the Clearwater Collection. One of the most interesting for its associations was fashioned *c.* 1710 by Peter van Inburgh for the Sill family from an earlier cup, won at a horse race on Long Island, and is inscribed on the bowl "1668 wunn: att hanpsted plaines march 25" (Garvan Collection). Daniel Denton in his 1670 description of Long Island states: "Towards the Middle of the island lyeth a plain 16 miles long and 4 broad, where you will find neither stick nor stone to hinder the horses heels or endanger them in their races, and once a year, the best horses in the land are brought hither to try their swiftness, and the swiftest rewarded with a silver cup." Apparently the cup became battered or for some unrecorded reason was consigned to the melting pot, but its earlier form memorialized in the inscription, a practice not uncommon in England.

The standing salt which had enjoyed the place of honor at table since mediaeval times lost out in this period to circular trencher salts, decorated with gadrooned bands on shoulder and base, which were usually made in pairs. No less than three pairs by Bartholomew LeRoux and Jacobus van der Spiegel, single ones by Koenraet Ten Eyck, and a Boston pair, one by John Coney, the other by Edward Winslow, have survived. The standing salts are found only in New England and the three surviving examples (Plate 10a) by Allen & Edwards, Jeremiah Dummer and Edward Winslow are spool-shaped, with top and base octagonal in section, decorated with vertical or spiral gadrooning, having four equidistant scrolled brackets at the top, presumably for the support of a dish. Casters made their appearance in a variety of forms, the most elegant being the set of three, with one larger than the other two. Cylindrical in form with flaring base ornamented with a gadrooned band, they have tall covers boldly pierced in geometric or floral pattern, enriched on the edge with gadrooning and surmounted by a turned finial (Plate 10b). Simple cylindrical boxes with perforated, slightly-domed cover and handle were popular for pepper. The earliest mustard pot (Plate 10c), fashioned by Peter van Dyck (1684–1750), has an egg-shaped body resting on a flaring foot decorated with a gadrooned band and border of stamped ornament (Garvan Collection).

Cider, beer, ale, wine, punch and rum continued in popularity as recorded by Madam Sarah Knight, who, on her journey from Boston to New York in 1704, was kept awake so late at Narragansett by noisy tipsters that she wrote in her journal—

> I ask thy Aid, O potent Rum,
> To charm these wrangling Topers Dum.

The beaker underwent little change from its seventeenth-century form other than the occasional use of an inverted bell-shaped body whose surbase was frequently decorated with a wide gadrooned and fluted band. The cover of the New England tankard was often enriched by the use of a spiral or vertical gadrooned band and the handle treated with a gadrooned effect. Surface variation was also achieved by the use of cut-card ornament in floral or leaf designs cut from a thin sheet of silver and applied on the cover or lower part of the body at the handle jointure. A charming variant in the cast thumbpiece is a pair of addorsed dolphins supporting a circular grinning mask, symbolic of strength and gaiety. The New York silversmiths continued to use the tankard form of the seventeenth century but one finds a refinement in the use of mouldings, applied foliated base bands and in the casting of the continuing cork-screw thumbpiece, as in the work of Jacobus van der Spiegel, Cornelius Kierstede, Benjamin Wynkoop and Peter van Dyck. The last achieved a rich effect by gadrooning, embossing and engraving the cover of an elaborate tankard exhibiting all the other typical New York characteristics (Plate 11). On wedding tankards the cast handle terminus depicts two figures with clasped hands. Oftentimes the original owners were women; Blandina Bayard in her will in 1711 leaves to her daughter Sarah "£12 in money to make her a silver tankard when she is of age or married." Mugs of quart and pint size followed the same general shape and decorative treatment of tankards in Boston and New York respectively.

Children's cups and spouted covered cups of globular shape with straight necks for feeding invalids are similar in form to the English glass version of the two-handled spouted and covered syllabub cup of the late seventeenth century. Most surviving examples have a single handle at right angles to the spout, but a unique two-handled example by Jeremiah Dummer is in the collection of the Museum of Fine Arts.

The generous two-handled punch bowl with decorated floral panels on its flaring sides continued in favor in New York, as examples by Cornelius Kierstede, Jesse Kip, and Benjamin Wynkoop testify. Caudle and sack posset remained favorite New England drinks and the shape of the vessel conformed to the prevailing style of bell-shaped body decorated with alternating spiral or vertical gadrooning and fluting; in fashioning these William Cowell (1682–1736) was particularly adept, judging from the surviving examples in church and museum collections.

The ceremony of health-drinking is vividly recalled by the imposing two-handled covered cups, two of which attest to the skill of their makers, John Coney and Edward Winslow. We are indebted to Judge Samuel Sewall for the circumstances surrounding the presentation to Harvard College of the one fashioned by Coney (Plate 12). In his Diary under date of 30 June, 1701, Sewall records his visit to the then ailing Lt. Governor William Stoughton:

Lt. Gov$^{r.}$ said would go to the Commencement once more in his life-time; so would adjourn the Court to Friday; and did so. But was very much pain'd going home. Mr. Nelson, Secretary and I visit him on Thursday to dissuade him from going, lest some ill consequence should happen. He consented, and order'd us to present his Bowl. After Dinner and singing, I took it, and had it fill'd up, and drunk to the president, saying that by reason of the absence of him who was the Firmament and Ornament of the Province, and that Society I presented that Grace-Cup pro more Academarium in Anglia.

The large covered cup by Winslow differs from that by Coney in that the scrolled handles are hollow, resembling those of tankards, and variation of surface pattern is effected by the use of vertical gadrooning on cover body and foot (Garvan Collection). The circular flat-topped salver which is usually found with these "grace" or "loving cups" retains the trumpet-shaped foot of its earlier form and is decorated with spiral or vertical gadrooned edges on tray and foot. Examples by John Coney, Jeremiah Dummer, John Allen & John Edwards, Edward Winslow and Jacobus van der Spiegel are known.

A novelty in the service of wine was a vessel introduced into England in the last quarter of the seventeenth century. It was apparently not originally intended for punch, but according to the English antiquary Anthony à Wood in 1683 was used as "a vessel or bason notched at the brim to let drinking glasses hang there by the foot so that the body and drinking place might hang in the water to cool them. Such a bason was a 'Monteigh,' from a fantastical Scot called 'Monsieur Monteigh,' who at that time or a little before wore the bottome of his cloake or coate so notched." A London example of 1705 was owned by the hospitable New Yorker, Abraham de Peyster, who served as alderman, mayor, President of the King's Council, Acting Governor of the Colony and first Treasurer of the Provinces of New York and New Jersey. This form may have been introduced into New York by the extravagant and eccentric Lord Cornbury, cousin-german to Queen Anne, who continually shocked New Yorkers by his escapades during his short term as Royal Governor. It is interesting to note from the receipts of Cornelius Kierstede and Benjamin Wynkoop and a claim of £130 7s. 4d. for plate from the less fortunate Bartholomew LeRoux, that Lord Cornbury patronized the New York silversmiths. The earliest monteith or cooler, as it was termed in an article appearing in *America Heraldica* (1865), is the superb example (Plate 13) fashioned by John Coney (Garvan Collection). Its deep, rounded, fluted bowl with notched rim, richly ornamented with cast scrolls, brackets and cherub-heads, rests on a gadrooned foot. Two cast panelled handles hang from finely modelled lion's heads. It varies from the contemporary English form in being much deeper, and lacks the embossed circular panel on the side reserved for a coat-of-arms, which distinguishes the English examples of the 1700–1710 period. On Coney's bowl, the arms are engraved on the inside on the bottom of the bowl, in itself an ingenious feat. It was fashioned for the wealthy merchant, John Colman, whose brother-in-law Charles Hobby was knighted by Queen Anne in 1705. In August of that year Colman was deputed receiver of the perquisites due "his Royal Highness Prince George of Denmark Lord High Admiral of Eng . . . in these parts." In May of the following year he was one of the Boston merchants petitioning the General Court to memorialize the Home Government to establish a monthly "Packett" from England to the New England colonies.

Indispensable in the luxurious service of liquors was the sugar box, an oval casket with hinged domed cover supported on four cast scrolled feet. The silversmith lavished all his skill on these, judging from the eight surviving examples, all from New England: three from Coney's workshop, four by Edward Winslow (1669–1753) and one by Daniel Greenough. The serving of sugar with sack had become well established in England by Shakespeare's time and its similar use in New England is revealed by Sewall, who speaks of Madam Winthrop treating him with a dram of black cherry brandy and a lump of sugar that was in it. Two of these boxes by Coney resemble closely a London example of 1676 and may have been inspired by an English example in Boston. Their frequent occurrence in seventeenth-century inventories has been noted in chapter two, and yet no English example with a Boston lineage is known today. The casket is decorated with a series of oval bosses, outlined by chasing, and the elaborate chased cover is decorated with leaves in relief against a matted ground with a handle in the form of a finely coiled

Plate 11

Significant features of this outstanding New York Baroque tankard by Van Dyck are the richly decorated cover, combining repoussé, chased and engraved ornament, foliated base band, and a cast handle ornament to ensure a good grip. Detail shows the Wendell arms, engraved on the front. Height 7⅛″

Plate 12

The harmonious effect of cast, chased, engraved, and repoussé ornament achieved by John Coney in his execution of Harvard College's magnificent two-handled covered cup in 1701 is evidence of the artist-craftsman's thorough understanding of his material, and his appreciation of proportion. Height 10"

serpent, symbolic of eternity. The four Winslow boxes, while varying slightly in execution of ornament and size are of similar design, unlike any known English counterpart. One of the outstanding features is the rich use of deep alternating gadrooning and fluting and the embossed representation of St. George and the dragon on the body of three of them. Of the three two bear the contemporarily engraved date of 1702. The one illustrated (Plate 14) was made by Winslow for his own family, in which it descended until its acquisition for the Garvan Collection.

The introduction of those luxuries, chocolate, tea and coffee, provided the silversmith with new forms, often influenced by the stylish and highly prized Oriental porcelain. Their shapes, expressing an Oriental idea of beauty to which the Western eye was unaccustomed, offered a fresh esthetic experience. This influence is found in the early chocolate pot with ogee-shaped body, narrowing at the base; its curved spout, decorated with graduate beading, is at right angles to the wooden handle, whose lower socket jointure is masked by cut-card ornament. The low domed cover's turned finial is removable for insertion of a rod to crush and stir the chocolate. The inscription on its bottom "The gift of Wm Stoughton Esquire, To Mrs Sarah Tailer: 701" refers to the clause in Lt. Governor Stoughton's will proved in 1701: "Unto my niece Mrs. Sarah Tailer I give as a particular remembrance of me twelve pounds to buy a piece of Plate." Her uncle's fondness for chocolate may have inspired this form of remembrance, as Sewall records in his Diary, 20 Oct. 1697: "I wait on the Lieut. Governour at Dorchester, and there meet with Mr. Torey, breakfast together on Venison and chockalatte." When Madam Sarah Knight made her now famous horseback journey from Boston to New York in 1704 she records providing the landlady at Havens Tavern with "some Chocolett . . . which with the help of some Milk, and a little clean brass Kettle, she soon effected to my satisfaction." Two chocolate pots (Plate 15) fashioned slightly later by Winslow differ in shape from this Coney one, having a tall tapering body, rounded at the base, with moulded foot and tall domical cover surmounted by a removable acorn finial; the lower part of body, cover, rim of cover and foot are decorated with vertical gadrooning. The spout on one is hammered and that on the other is cast, but both are placed at right angles to the handle. A third similar in form, by Peter Oliver (1682–1712), is also known.

Tea, which had long enjoyed popularity in Holland, was apparently introduced in New York earlier than in Boston. The early pots are based on the Chinese porcelain wine or water pots used in pouring the hot water over the leaves in cups; tea was not infused in the pot as in the Occidental world. The earliest American example is a globular pot (Plate 16) with a straight spout and detached gadrooned and embossed cover fashioned by Jacob Boelen (1654–1729). The delightful bit of stamped ornament on its base is reminiscent of the New York beakers and proclaims its provenance as do the engraved arms of its owner, Frederick Philipse, a merchant engaged in the Madagascar trade. His opulence in 1698 is indicated in Lord Bellomont's report to the London Board of Trade: "When Frederick Phillipp's ship and the other two come from Madagascar (which are expected every day) New York will abound with gold."

Alcoholic and non-alcoholic beverages were prepared and kept hot in a chafing dish of cylindrical body with an everted rim boldly pierced in a scrolled design. Three scrolled projections above the rim terminate in claws grasping wooden balls for insulation purposes. Above the solid bottom a moulded rim supports a bolted pierced disc on which the burning charcoal was placed. A pair by Coney in the Pickman Collection are the sole known survivors.

A candlestick by Coney, circular in plan with baluster stem and decorated with gadrooning, is also in the same collection. The more common form shows an architectural influence in the use of a fluted column resting on a square or octagonal base enriched with gadrooning; three privately owned imposing pairs by John Noyes, Henricus Boelen and Cornelius Kierstede have survived. The pair by Kierstede is unique in its engraved bizarre ornament *à la chinoiserie*, popular in England during the late seventeenth century, and in having an equally elaborate matching snuffer stand, now in the collection of the Metropolitan Museum of Art.

One should not overlook such small personal items of silver as shoe buckles, buttons, engraved circular, oval and heart-shaped boxes for

Plate 13

The most ambitious surviving piece by an American silversmith is Coney's monteith. Although based on an English form, it differs widely from any known English example. The influence of Baroque architectural ornament is evident in the Colman arms engraved in the bottom. Diameter 11"

Plate 14

Exotic in contrast to the simplicity associated with the silver of New England are the elaborate sugar boxes, popular in the late 17th and early 18th centuries, attesting to the manipulative skill of the craftsman. Winslow fashioned this one for his own family. Length 7½"

tobacco, snuff and ladies' patches, and the rare articles in gold, including buttons and lockets with richly engraved surfaces, as well as thimbles, chains, and those enormous quantities of rings presented to chief mourners and ministers at funerals, often chased with a winged skull and bearing on the interior the deceased's name, age and date of death.

The use of such bold ornamentation as the gadroon required an equally bold eye-arresting pattern in heraldic engraving. This was accomplished by treating the acanthus-leaf mantling of the preceding period with rounder and more whorling effects, as on the Stoughton arms engraved by Coney and Dummer in 1701 on the Harvard loving cup and the Dorchester standing cups, or by the use of embossing as on the Winslow sugar box (1702) in Mrs. Edsel Ford's Collection. The New York style continued in an even more florid manifestation of their seventeenth-century formula as evidenced by Peter van Dyck's engraving of the Wendel arms on the tankard (Plate 11) in the Garvan Collection or Jacob Boelen's rendering of the Philipse arms on the teapot in Mrs. Lloyd Garrison's possession (Plate 16). Around 1711, a new style of heraldic ornament was introduced, not based upon heraldic form but inspired by contemporary architectural ornament, in which the device is displayed on the oval panel of a baroque scrolled cartouche. The earliest dated examples occur on the rim of three dishes engraved with the Hutchinson and Foster arms, fashioned by Edward Winslow in 1711 for the Second Church, Boston. To this same period may be assigned on stylistic grounds the Colman arms engraved by Coney in the base of the earliest known American monteith (Plate 13, Garvan Collection).

The delightful counterpoise of plain and boldly ornamental surfaces and the balance maintained between intricate design and perfection of workmanship, as manifested in the surviving pieces of this short period, usher in the golden age of American silversmithing at a time when the centers of the craft had yet to celebrate their centenary.

GREENE

Chapter four

Transplanted Queen Anne, 1715-1750

FEAR OF A SHORTAGE OF COINAGE RESULTING FROM THE fashionable wholesale melting down of coins for conversion into plate, which had begun in the reign of Charles II and continued into the reign of William and Mary, necessitated the passage of an Act by Parliament in 1697 raising the cost of the raw material. Under the terms of this Act, the standard of purity for plate was raised from the Sterling of 11 oz. 2 dwt. pure silver in each troy pound to 11 oz. 10 dwt. The order had the desired effect and by 1720 the old Sterling standard was restored. Largely as a result of the increased softness of the metal under the new standard, the elaborate embossed forms were not practical and were gradually replaced by forms whose simplicity of line and graceful shape were enhanced by fine mouldings, facets and cast ornament. This style, associated with Queen Anne, did not become universally popular until the year of her death and continued through the reign of her successor George I. Although the law was not enforced in Scotland or Ireland, the silver styles in those countries were modified in accordance with the prevailing London fashions. In much the same way the style was adopted in the colonies, where it became extremely popular. It should be said that the popularity of plain undecorated silver had never been completely eclipsed in the preceding period in either England or the colonies, so the great popularity enjoyed by this style, particularly in Boston, might be argued as the indigenous growth of the Puritan tradition.

Closer contacts with England, and the influence of the changing modes of wig, dress, and furniture are reflected in the colonies by the time of the death of Queen Anne. Daniel Neal, observing the adoption by the Bostonians of English fashions, wrote in 1718: "The Conversation in this Town is as polite as in most of the cities and towns of England; many of their Merchants having travell'd into Europe; and those that stay at home having the Advantage of a free Conversation with Travellers, so that a Gentleman from London would almost think himself at home in Boston when he observes the Numbers of People, their Houses, their Furniture, their Tables, their Dress and Conversation which perhaps is as splendid and showy, as that of the most considerable Tradesman in London . . . in the Concerns of Civil Life, as in their Dress, Tables and Conversation, they affect to be as much English as possible, there is no Fashion in London, but three or four Months is to be seen here at Boston, nay, they are fond of the very Name and Person of an English man." A year later, Thomas Amory wrote: "People live handsomely here [Boston] and without fear of anything." This continued interest in luxury in Puritan Boston had indeed alarmed the old guard, and when Peter Pelham attempted to introduce a dancing assembly disapproval was expressed by an anonymous anti-social writer in the *Boston Gazette* of 5 April 1734 in the statement: "It is too well known how our Extravagance in Apparel and Luxury at our Tables, are hastening the ruin of our Country, and are evils which call loudly for a remedy."

These statements are substantiated by the contemporary inventories, with their greater number and variety of silver forms, indicating a considerable interest in increased domestic comfort. Governor William Burnet, who died at Boston in 1728, left a considerable quantity of silver which was weighed and appraised by the Boston silversmith, Edward Winslow. Among the pieces listed are:

12 candlesticks, 2 branches for 3 lights, 1 snuff dish and snuffers, 3 stands and 3 pair snuffers, 3 castors and crewit stand, pepper box, 8 salts, 2 canns, chaffendish and plate, a large Square Salver, 4 small ditto, 1 shaving bason, 2 two-handled porringers, 1 Sangarey

[punch] Cup and cover, 1 Mountef [Monteith], 2 large decanters, 2 coffee pots, Teapot, small panneken with wooden handle, 2 doz. and 16 spoons, 8 teaspoons, tea tongs, 3 soup ladles, 1 punch spoon, pr. spurs, 2 pr. shoe buckles, 2 pr. garter buckles, child's spoon, toothpick case, large silver gilt salver, 4 silver gilt antient family Cups with Covers, 6 gilt tea Spoons, pr. tongs and strainer, doz. spoons, doz. knives, doz. forks, for a Desert, three cases containing 3 doz. knives and 3 doz. forkes with silver handles.

Winslow also appraised the plate the following year in the estate of Madam Mary Saltonstall, widow of Governor Gurdon Saltonstall of Connecticut. In it are listed: 1 pair of candlesticks, 1 snuffer and stand, 1 sugar box & spoon, pair of casters, 6 forks, 2 salvers, 7 spoons, 5 tea-spoons, 1 pair of tongs, 1 egg strainer, 1 small tankard, 1 pair chafing dishes, 1 inkcase, 1 grater & case, 4 salts, 1 porringer, 2 salvers, a teapot and lamp, a large cup with wood handles, a large cup with a cover, 1 large bason, all weighing 329 oz. 4 dwt. which at 18s. per ounce was valued at £296 5s. 7¼d. More pertinent is a list made in 1728 by the Harvard tutor Nicholas Sever, for of the 12 known pieces of hollow-ware, all were fashioned within the period. The "Invoice" dated April 6, 1728, lists: "A two Quart Tankard, A Quart Tankard, A pair of Chafing dishes, A pair of Candlesticks, two Salvers, A Large and a Small one, A pair of Canns, two Porringers, A Tea Pot, two Salts, four Spoons, Six Teaspoons, Six more wth Tongs & Strainer, Two Spoons more."

The introduction here of this new style undoubtedly came through the royal gifts by Queen Anne of ecclesiastical plate to the leading Episcopal Churches in the colonies. The earliest evidence in American plate is to be found in the two-handled church cups of plain bell-shape body with two strap handles and moulded foot, the first of which was fashioned in 1714 by John Dixwell (1680–1725), son of the Regicide Judge of the same name who sought refuge in New Haven upon the restoration of Charles II. It is difficult to determine whether the style of this cup derives from an indigenous growth, since there are no similar cups in English silver, or is the result of Dixwell's impression of the plain styles during his visit to England in 1710. Simple bell-shaped beakers, on a low moulded foot, enriched by beautifully engraved inscriptions, and tall domed covered flagons with cast bell-shaped finials, scrolled

Plate 15

Winslow's chocolate pot demonstrates his fine understanding of balance between plain and richly ornamented surfaces, employing gadrooned and cut-card decoration. Height $9\frac{1}{8}$"

a) *The richly ornamented separate cover, straight spout, bulbous shape, foot, and elaborately engraved Philipse arms on this teapot by Jacob Boelen mark it as an example of early Dutch New York craftsmanship. Height 6¼"*

b) *A significant feature of the teapot by Peter van Dyck, based on Dutch form, is the use on the cover of applied strap-work ornament, popular with the Anglo-French silversmiths of London and New York. Height 8"*

thumbpieces and simple handles together with plain broad-rimmed baptismal basins complete the chief types made for the churches. Parishioners still continued to leave to their minister or their church a large percentage of their tankards, caudle cups, etc., many of which have unfortunately been melted. In conservative New York, the seventeenth-century beaker shape continued in popularity as late as 1731, judging by a pair of surviving examples fashioned in that year by Henricus Boelen (1697–1755) for the Reformed Church of near-by Bergen, New Jersey.

Flatware, appearing in sets, featured a new spoon, the rounded end of whose handle was upcurved and thickened with a prominent ridge running down its front. The plain rat-tail continues on the back of the bowl until about 1730 when it is discarded in favor of a double drop or shell in relief (Plate 2b). With the disappearance of the rat-tail, the ridge on the handle front becomes less pronounced. Spoons were made in three sizes, to which was added the strainer spoon with pierced bowl useful for removing stray leaves from tea or seeds from punch. Eight gold teaspoons from a set of twelve and a strainer spoon of this pattern fashioned by Simeon Soumain (1685–1750) for a Barbadoes planter are among the treasures of the Garvan Collection (Plate III). Large basting spoons follow the same pattern, as do forks, which are numbered among the rarities in American silver. Hollow-handled ladles for punch were supplemented by ladles with double-lipped bowls and turned wooden handles.

The porringer became increasingly popular in all localities and the earliest examples of this period in Boston and Philadelphia have a simplified geometric pattern consisting of graceful scrolls. In 1725 a handle of pierced scrolls enclosing an elongated opening at the apex, to which the term "keyhole" has been given, made its appearance. The earlier versions of this type have two arched openings on the handle plate near the bowl, but these disappear by 1740. This handle style, with slight variations, became popular in Boston, Newport, Philadelphia, and even New York, although in the latter city there was a preference for a broad handle pierced with three simple openings (Page 89), a style which, probably through trade, is found on an occasional Newport piece. A covered example by John Brevoort (1715–1775) is in the Garvan Collection.

Associated with the porringer for feeding children, women in childbirth, and the infirm is the increasingly popular spout-cup which had made its appearance in the preceding period. The earlier ones had a bulbous body, domed finial covers with finely cast handles at right angles to the high duck-neck spouts, as in the examples by John Coney and Nathaniel Morse. A few beaker-shaped examples without covers by Edward Winslow and his nephew Moody Russell have been noted. Those dating after 1720 have a pear-shaped body, slightly domed cover, with small finial, and strap handle at right angles to the spout. Examples by Andrew Tyler, Samuel Edwards, William Cowell, Bartholomew Green and Benjamin Hiller have survived. Only one example with the spout opposite the handle is known; it was fashioned by Joseph Richardson, Sr. (1711–1784) (Collection of Mr. and Mrs. Walter M. Jeffords).

Trencher salts with moulded and splayed sides, oval or octagonal in section, are found as late as 1730, at which time they were replaced by circular salts with moulded rim supported on three cabriole legs terminating in pad or toed feet, a style reminiscent of Queen Anne furniture. Casters in sets of three for sugar and spices are found in panelled, pear-shaped and vase-shaped forms, resting on moulded feet, with beautifully pierced and engraved covers, surmounted by finely cast finials. Small octagonal boxes with moulded rim and base, pierced cover and a strap handle were used for pepper. The angular forms and polygonal shapes employed in these casters and pepper boxes (Plate 17a) enhance the beauty of the metal's rich surface.

Sauce or butter boats were introduced during this period, the earliest survivors follow the French shape of low oval body, scalloped rim with two lips and handles, resting on an oval foot. Such a pair was fashioned by Charles LeRoux of New York. A more popular shape had a broad body with long everted lip, shaped rim, high scrolled handle, and rested on three hoof feet like those on contemporary chairs and silver salts.

The chafing dish, still a comparative rarity in English plate, is found in great numbers, often in pairs, with and without turned wooden handles. The curved basin pierced in a variety of designs has an everted lip and three scrolled bracket supports; early in the period the supports

Plate III

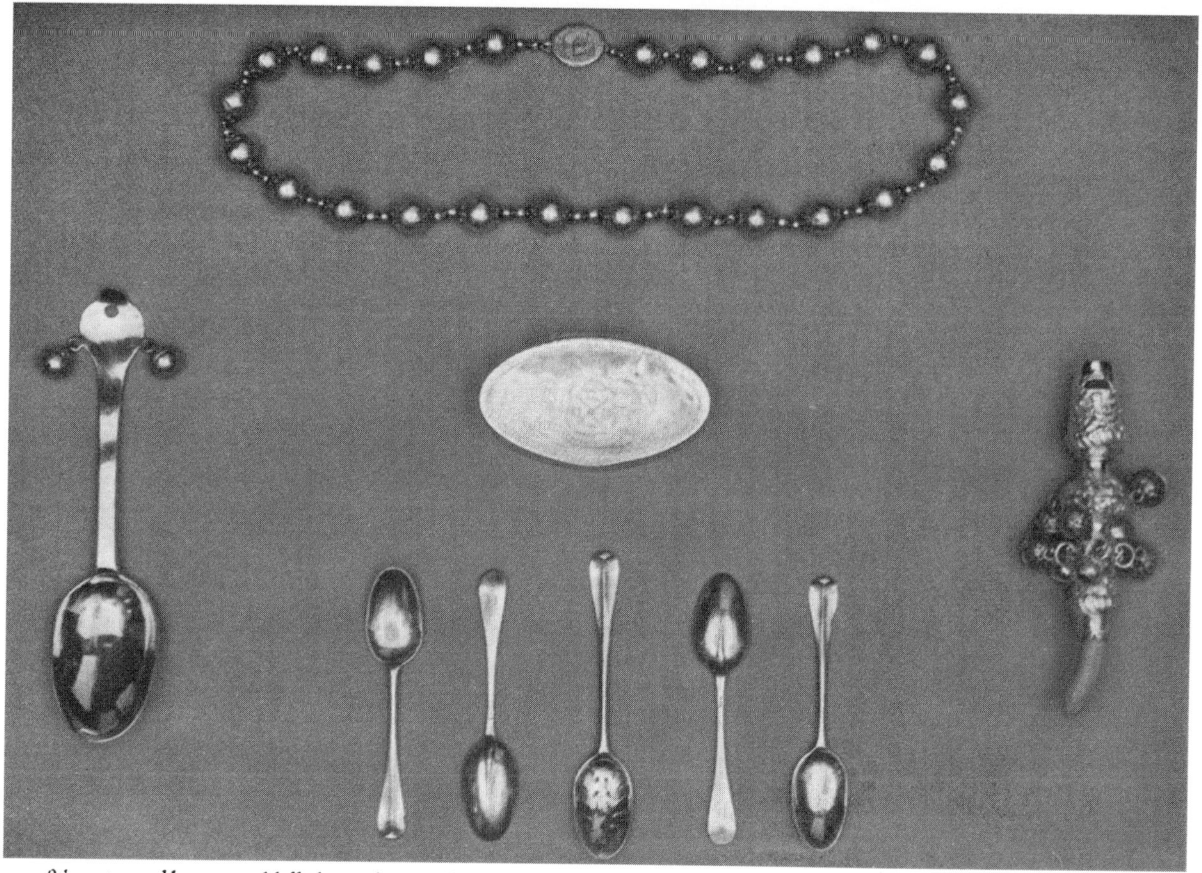

18th-century gold: spoon and bells by Jacobus van der Spiegel; teaspoons and strainer spoon by Simeon Soumain; necklace by Peter van Dyck; "freedom box" by Samuel Johnson; rattle by Daniel Christian Fueter

terminated in silver claws grasping wooden balls, but these were in turn discarded in favor of the hoof foot of salt, sauceboat and bowl supports. Among those who worked in the earlier style and whose examples have survived may be mentioned John Coney (Plate 17c), John Burt, Nathaniel Morse, Edward Winslow of Boston, Peter van Dyck of New York, and Johannis Nys of Philadelphia. Prominent among those silversmiths employing the cast silver hoof foot are John Burt, Jacob Hurd, Thomas Edwards and Joseph Kneeland. Of these, John Burt had in 1724 fashioned a pair in the earlier style, employing the claw foot and wooden ball as tutorial plate for Nicholas Sever, another evidence of the craftsman's ability to change his pattern to suit the times.

The cider tankard's popularity is attested not only by the large number that have survived but by the distinctive treatment it received in the various silversmithing centers. Early in the period Boston favored a tankard with slightly more tapering body, moulded base, domed cover with or without a turned finial, scrolled thumbpiece, plain handle ending in an oval boss or cast cherub's-head tip. This was soon discarded for a type having a quarter-round moulding encircling the body below the middle, with a flattened domed cover with or without a bell-shaped finial. On two examples by Coney, the thumbpiece is in the form of a finely cast eagle with spread wings, a feature also used by Samuel Vernon of Newport. The Rhode Islanders fancied a tankard with a tapering body and a domed cover decorated with a bell-shaped finial, but no Rhode Island tankard bearing a mid-band is known to the writer. The New Yorkers retained the flat-topped tankard with corkscrew thumbpiece, and in a few instances even the applied foliated band—although there are many examples with a plain moulded base. The scrolled thumbpiece is found after 1745 but in conjunction with the flat cover. Philadelphia tankards are closer to contemporary London styles, having domed covers on tapering bodies, plain or decorated with a mid-band without the use of a finial. By 1730, the body of the tankard becomes rounded at the base, and the simple hammered scroll handle is replaced by a cast handle of double scroll form. These innovations can be seen in the work of Philip Syng, Jr., who, following his apprenticeship in the 1720's, had spent part of a year in England, which may account for this novel treatment. Both the Philadelphia and New York tankards present a sturdier appearance than those of New England.

Mugs followed the general form of the tankard, but lost their popularity following the introduction of the cann, a drinking vessel, usually of pint capacity, with curved sides and rounded bottom, resting on a low moulded foot, with single or double scrolled handle. Small beaker-shaped cups with simple moulded base and strap, or cast handle, decorated with graduated beading, were extremely popular, particularly as gifts for children.

The most imposing piece of plate was the large two-handled covered cup; the earliest example, by Coney, a present from Harvard students in 1718 to tutor Henry Flynt, has a plain bell-shaped body on a moulded splayed foot, two cast scroll handles and a domed and moulded cover with turned finial. The only decoration on its surface is the Flynt arms neatly engraved on one side and the presentation inscription on the other. A larger example by John Burt in the Harvard College Collection shows that this form continued in style as late as 1731. Some time before 1744, the plain surface of such cups was enriched by the addition of the mid-band as, for example, on Jacob Hurd's masterpiece, commissioned as a presentation piece for a naval victory (Garvan Collection). The quality of its scale mouldings and its handsomely cast curved handles show Hurd's grasp of proportion and balance. Its sole decoration, save for the moulding that girdles it, is the legend fittingly inscribed against a trophy of arms

To/EDWARD TYNG Esq./Commander of ye SNOW/Prince of Orange/As an acknowledgement of/his good Service done the/TRADE in Taking ye First/French Privateer/ on this Coast the 24th day of June/1744. This Plate is presented/BY several of ye Merch^{ts}/ in Boston New England

which vividly recalls the early encounter between a snow, a type of warship, built at the expense of the Massachusetts Bay Colony to protect her fisheries, and a French privateer at the outbreak of King George's War (Plate II). At the time of presentation, it was used, according to contemporary records, as a container for "Bishop," a sweet drink made of wine, oranges, or lemons and sugar with mulled and spiced port. A similar cup of different proportions was made by Hurd for the prominent

Plate 17

a) *Soumain's sugar caster, engraved with the Maddox arms, is an excellent example of the octagonal form, whose popularity spread to tea sets and lighting fixtures during the Queen Anne period. Height* $7\frac{1}{2}''$

b) *Philip Syng's engraving of the Maddox arms on a tankard demonstrates the symmetry and balance of the framework as well as the "imbrication" in the lining*

c) *A Coney chafing dish, made for his own family, demonstrates the quality of pierced geometric ornament in the Queen Anne period. Diameter* $5\frac{5}{16}''$

Plate 18

a) *Punch bowl with flat-chased ornament in Kierstede's distinctive style was a gift of Yale students in 1745 to their tutor, Thomas Darling. Diameter* $7\frac{1}{2}''$

b) *"Jacobean" heraldic engraving and the supporting cabriole legs, closely related to contemporary furniture forms, are the distinguishing features of this punch bowl by John Burt. Diameter 7"*

Boston merchant, John Rowe, in this decade (Museum of Fine Arts). One of similar shape by William Swan was presented to Benjamin Pickman in 1749 by the Province of Massachusetts for his aid in promoting the successful expedition against Louisburg (Essex Institute, Salem). Two examples made in New York by Charles LeRoux (1689–1745) in their decoration of applied petal-shaped strap work on body and cover reflect a modified interpretation of a form popular in London with the Anglo-French silversmiths.

Plain punch bowls with simple curving sides, moulded rim and foot, were popular and such a one fashioned by John Inch (1720–1763) of Annapolis, inscribed "Annapolis Subscription Plate 4 May 1743," was won by Dr. George Steuart's horse, Dungannon (Baltimore Museum of Art). Punch bowls were also a favorite racing prize in Boston: in the *Boston News Letter*, May 15/22, 1721, it was advertised that "On the 2^d. of June next at 4 in the afternoon, A Silver Punch Bowl Value Ten Pounds will be run for on Cambridge Heath, Three Miles by any Horse, Mare or Gelding 13 hands, 3 inches High, none to exceed 14, carrying Nine Stone Weight, if any Horse is 14 hand high to carry Ten Stone weight, The Horses that put in for the Plate are to Enter at the Post Office in Boston on the 1st of June between the hours of 8 & 12 in the morning, and pay down Twenty Shillings. The winning Horse to pay the charge of the Advertisement."

The only surviving punch bowl of tutorial plate is one fashioned by Cornelius Kierstede (1675–1757) long after his removal from New York to New Haven, where he combined in his individualistic way the Queen Anne outline with the New York panelled floral patterns, executed in flat-chasing. This piece (Plate 18a) was the gift of the class of 1746 to their sole tutor, Thomas Darling, upon the occasion of his retirement in 1745, and now appropriately forms a part of the Yale University Collection. An interesting bowl and a variant in form is that (Plate 18b) fashioned by John Burt and now in the collection of Mr. and Mrs. Walter M. Jeffords. Its plain, curved body, richly engraved with the arms and names of six prominent Boston merchants, rests on three hoof feet. Unfortunately the circumstances of its origin are unknown but it is to be hoped that through a study of the engraving its early associations can be discovered. One example of the monteith fashioned for a New York family in the Boston workshop of John Coney has survived from this period. It has a plain, deep body with scalloped moulded rim, originally removable, and a moulded foot. It is engraved with the Livingston arms on the bowl and with the cypher R.A.L., standing for its original owners, Robert and Alida Livingston, on the rim above the arms; it is now owned by their descendant, Mrs. Henry Parish.

Taste for chocolate seems to have been on the wane, as only two pots, both from Boston, have survived. The earliest, by Coney, has a pear-shaped body ornament with cut-card work, moulded foot, cast duck-neck spout terminating in a bird's beak and domed cover surmounted by a turned finial. Somewhat later is that by Zachariah Brigden employing the lantern shape with moulded base, rim and domed cover, a form popular for coffee pots; the only point of difference is the removable top, permitting insertion of the stirring rod. Coffee pots of plain lantern shape dating from this period by John Burt, and Jacob Hurd of Boston, Charles LeRoux and Peter van Dyck of New York, Peter David and Joseph Richardson, Sr., of Philadelphia, have survived. All examples, except that by LeRoux, have curved spouts opposite wooden handles; LeRoux's has a straight spout at right angles to its wooden handle.

The popularity of tea, with its special tables and imported china involving elaborate ceremony, stimulated the production of new silver forms. When Joseph Bennett visited Boston in 1740 he wrote: "The ladies here visit, drink tea and indulge every little piece of gentility to the height of the mode and neglect the affairs of their families with as good grace as the finest ladies in London." The earliest Boston teapot, by Coney, is pear-shaped with high domed cover, knob finial, duck-neck spout and curved wooden handle (Clearwater Collection). By 1728, the globular pot, inspired by ceramic forms, with flat hinged cover, wooden knob finial, moulded foot and octagonal spout was in fashion, as can be seen in the one presented in that year to tutor Nicholas Sever by his Harvard students. The flat cover and rim of these pots offered a surface suitable for finely engraved bands of ornament. A charming example

(Plate 19) by Jacob Hurd (1702–1758), fashioned for Sir William Pepperell, hero of Louisburg, dates from this time (Garvan Collection). A pleasing variation is the use of faceted forms on the spout. Numerous examples by John Burt, Thomas Edwards, Jacob Hurd, Paul Revere, Sr., attest to the popularity of this shape. The New Yorkers, consistently conservative, preferred the capacious pear-shaped form with high domed cover and cast scrolled polygonal spout—"the motherly teapot," as Washington Irving so aptly describes it in *The Legend of Sleepy Hollow*. In shape it is quite close to Dutch forms. Two early examples by Peter van Dyck employ on their covers an applied strap-work decoration, popular in French and Anglo-French silver. The great majority rely solely upon form and mouldings for their beauty, as examples by Peter van Dyck, Henricus Boelen, Adrian Banckner and John Brevoort indicate. The influence of the popular Dutch treatment of this shape, octagonal in plan, was reflected here not only in such a piece as that by van Dyck in the Garvan Collection but also in such an advertisement as the following:

This is to give Notice to all Gentlemen and others, That a Lottery is to be drawn at Mr. *John Stevens* in *Perth Amboy*, for £501 of Silver and Gold work, wrought by *Simeon Soumain* of *New York*, Gold-Smith, all of the newest Fashion. The highest Prize consists of an Eight square Tea-Pot, six Tea-Spoons, Skimmer and Tongues, Valued at £18 3s. 6d. . . . Tickets are given out at Six Shillings York money, or Seven Shillings Jersey Money for each Ticket . . . and by *Simeon Soumain* in the *City* of *New York*, at which last Place, the Goods so to be drawn are to be seen, and the said Goods are to be valued and apprised by Mr. *Peter van Dyck*, and Mr. *Charles Leroux*, two Gold Smiths in the City of *New York*. [*American Weekly Mercury*, March 23, 1727.]

The sugar dish and cream or milk jug became popular accessories for the European and American tea table. The shape of the former is based upon the china tea bowl of the Orient; its footed bowl with everted rim is surmounted by a low domed cover with reel-shaped handle. Among the most charming for sheer beauty of line is one (Plate 20a) that was fashioned for Elizabeth Cruger and bears her cypher neatly engraven on bowl and cover by Simeon Soumain (Garvan Collection). With slight stylistic differences, examples by the Bostonians Jacob Hurd, John Burt and John Coburn, by New Yorkers Adrian Banckner, Henricus Boelen and London-trained George Ridout, and by Philip Syng, Jr., of Philadelphia are known. A unique example is the oblong octagonal shaped dish fashioned by Jacob Hurd (Museum of Fine Arts, Boston).

The earliest surviving cream jugs have a pear-shaped body, pinched triangular spout, simple scrolled handle and plain, collared foot, usually with domed hinged covers and turned finials. This type was succeeded by a jug of more elongated body, with a longer and broader lip, double scrolled handle, having for support three cast cabriole or bandy legs ending in feet similar to contemporary furniture. One of the most popular of the Philadelphia silversmiths, Joseph Richardson, Sr., whose account books for the period 1733–40 are in the collection of the Historical Society of Pennsylvania, records making "eight square milk pots." The prevalence of drinking milk with tea in England is referred to by Matthew Prior in his poem "To A Young Gentleman in Love":

> He kissed her on his bended knee;
> Then drank a quart of milk and tea.

The surviving cream jugs from New York and Philadelphia, while following the same general shape, are a little chunkier than those of Boston.

The earliest known American kettle has a pear-shaped body consistent with the early form of the teapot, a flattened domed cover with a floral finial and a highly decorative spout that demonstrates the great originality of its maker, Cornelius Kierstede, who fashioned it for the de Peyster family. Its silver-mounted swinging handle of generously turned cherrywood, cut-card ornament and meandering wire along the rim create a piece which one can truly call American in style (Metropolitan Museum of Art). Closer to the English style is a privately owned globular example made by Jacob Hurd with faceted spout and swinging silver handle originally covered with a wicker grip. Its finely cast stand with scroll supports has today a lamp of later addition.

Among other new forms introduced in the service of tea was the canister or caddy, a corruption of *kati*, a Malay measure, as a container for tea. Found in sets of three, with the largest for sugar, one complete and

Plate 19

Sir William Pepperell's teapot, engraved with his arms, by Jacob Hurd shows a form, inspired by a Chinese ceramic shape, popular in Boston during the Queen Anne period. Height 5"

Plate 20

a) *Chinese tea bowls inspired this sugar dish with its characteristic reel-shaped handle and foot, a form which became universally popular in the Queen Anne period. This example, fashioned by Simeon Soumain for Elizabeth Cruger, bears her cypher engraved on bowl and cover. Height 4¼"*

b) *Triangular inkstand by John Coney, fashioned for Governor Belcher, is supported by finely modeled recumbent lions and is the earliest known American inkstand. Height 4¼"*

one incomplete set of American make have survived. The earlier, octagonal in plan, with moulded base and domed cover, was fashioned in New York by Simeon Soumain for the Bayard family. Two canisters by Thauvet Besley, also of New York, have rectangular bodies with incurved corners, moulded base and domed covers. The top of one is engraved "Bohea Tea"; that of the other "Green Tea." A set of three with oval bodies, made in London 1737–38, 1738–39, a gift to Sir William Pepperell by his partner in victory, Admiral Sir Peter Warren, remained in America until the Revolutionary War when it was taken to England along with a great quantity of plate; it is still in the possession of Sir William's descendants.

The salver with moulded flat circular top and trumpet foot is found early in this period. Two of different sizes were fashioned by John Burt in 1724 and 1728 for tutor Sever and are listed in the inventory which has been quoted earlier in this chapter. Other makers of this form were John Blowers, Ephraim Cobb, John Coney, Jacob Hurd, and John Potwine, Boston; Benjamin Wynkoop, Jr., Stratford, Connecticut; Charles LeRoux, New York; Johannis Nys and Henry Pratt, Philadelphia. A unique treatment by Edward Winslow occurs in one example with a trefoil-shaped top (Art Institute, Chicago). These were still used in the service of wine. Low-footed salvers for the use of coffee and tea equipage offer a variety of patterns, ranging from those of square form with curved rim and bracket feet or of rectangular form with incurved corners and scrolled feet to circular and polygonal shapes having beautifully moulded cast borders of sinuous lines that antedate the furniture forms popular after 1750. Joseph Richardson, Sr., fashioned such a one for Mary Grafton in 1746 "to weigh 8 oz. when Done" (Garvan Collection). Today it tips the scales at 7 oz. 12 dwt., a normal loss after the wear of two centuries. Among Richardson's contemporaries who expressed their skill and ingenuity in these forms may be mentioned Josiah Austin, Jacob Hurd and Charles LeRoux.

The introduction of secretary bookcases, with candle slides, as well as the popularity of gaming tables, is reflected in the numbers and variety of surviving lighting fixtures. The candlestick, which had previously been raised, is now cast in moulds. The earliest form, exemplified by a circular pair with baluster stem made by Coney, was varied by him in 1716 in a pair made for Tutor Flynt; this was polygonal in section, with faceted ornament enriching foot and socket of the baluster stem. A pair, octagonal in section, presented to Harvard tutor Nicholas Sever, inscribed "Donum Pupillorum 1724," now owned by Harvard University, was fashioned by John Burt, who shortly after also made a charming lighting set consisting of a pair of candlesticks, snuffer and oval-shaped tray supported on four pad feet. The frequency of baluster forms with square bases and incurved or canted corners, popular in England, has been noted in the works of the New Yorkers, Simeon Soumain, his apprentice William Anderson, Bartholomew Schaats, John Hastier, and London-trained George Ridout, who may have been responsible for the introduction of the style. An extremely rare type in American lighting fixtures is the pair of sconces with simple curving tubular arms and socket fitting into a circular plate, that could be affixed to a wooden frame of quill-work, fashioned by Knight Leverett (1703–1753) (Henry F. du Pont Collection).

Another rarity in American silver is the inkstand, or, as it was known, the standish. The earliest (Plate 20b) was fashioned by that master craftsman, John Coney, for politically-minded Jonathan Belcher, who served as Governor successively in the colonies of Massachusetts & New Hampshire and New Jersey. Its simple triangular tray with moulded edge contains three cylindrical receptacles for ink, sand (the forerunner of blotting paper), and wafers—with which the folded letter was sealed before the introduction of the envelope—grouped around a ringed baluster handle. The stand is supported by three finely cast and finished recumbent lions (Metropolitan Museum of Art).

Tobacco and snuff boxes, oval in plan, were extremely popular and in some instances the silversmith mounted tortoiseshell and mother-of-pearl with charming effect. The custom of pipe-smoking by ladies in Philadelphia is referred to in 1747 by diarist John Smith, when, on taking leave of B. Wyatt's wife, he presented "her with a Large pearl Tobacco Box set in silver In hopes of being remembred by when she

Plate IV

John Singleton Copley's portrait of Nathaniel Hurd (1730-77), famous Boston engraver of trade-cards and bookplates, silversmith and engraver of inscriptions and heraldic ornament. On the table beside him is one of the chief sources of his armorial designs, Guillim's "Display of Heraldry"

smoakes a pipe." One pleasing Marblehead lady, long since forgotten, received from her swain an oval engraved snuff box fashioned by William Jones (1694–1730), with this flattering inscription encircling its cover:

My love is fixt i wil not Range
i like my Choyce too well to Change.

Nor should one overlook the rare, oval gold snuff box fashioned by Jacob Hurd for the Lieutenant Governor of Massachusetts, William Dummer, and handsomely engraved with his arms (Museum of Fine Arts). Similar in shape is the gold "freedom" box, engraved with arms of the City of New York, and fashioned by Charles LeRoux in 1735. Such boxes were the customary municipal gifts accompanying the document presenting the freedom of the city to distinguished personages. This box was presented to Andrew Hamilton for his noble defense of John Peter Zenger in the trial by which freedom of the press was established in America (Historical Society of Pennsylvania).

These same two craftsmen were selected to fashion the silver oars of the Vice-Admiralty Courts in their respective localities. The silver oar or "mace" of the Marshal of the Court of Vice-Admiralty was the outward symbol of the authority which the court derived from the Crown to arrest both persons and vessels on the high seas; it was laid on the table before the Judge of the Court when he sat in judgment and carried before condemned pirates on their way to the gallows. These oars are approximately 23 inches in length; the court's name is on the handle, and the blade is engraved on one side with the Royal Arms of England and on the other with the Admiralty Anchor.

Among the personal items fashioned by the silversmith of this period are seals, knee and shoe buckles, octagonal sleeve buttons in both gold and silver, gold funeral and wedding rings, lockets and thimbles. Reminiscent of the gentle art of duelling are the surviving rapier hilts executed by John Coney, William Cowell, Jacob Hurd, Andrew Tyler and Edward Winslow.

The generous plain surfaces of the Queen Anne style invited fine engraving and in no other period did this branch of the silversmith's art approach such technical skill. It is likely that one source of many of the cyphers engraved within a double-lined circle is to be found in Sympson's *Book of Cyphers* published in London, particularly as two of the engravers attesting to its usefulness settled in the colonies, Peter Pelham at Boston in 1728 and Bishop Roberts at Charleston by 1735. That imported plate also served as a model is indicated by surviving pieces owned originally by the Pennsylvania Provincial Council member and William Penn's secretary, James Logan. A tankard of his, fashioned by Johannis Nys (Collection, Mrs. Maurice Brix), bears a bold rendering of the same cypher and framework as was neatly engraved on his fashionable tea service, traditionally ordered for him in London by his friend, William Penn.

The advertisements in the newspapers from 1740 to 1748 of engravers just arrived from London, engraving "in the best Manner, and after the Newest fashion, in Gold, Silver or any kind of Metal, Coats of Arms," suggest a source of these beautifully executed designs which has not, as yet, been fully investigated. The conventional heraldic form of shield, helmet, crest and mantling was largely discarded in favor of a design popular in contemporary English silver as well as in the so-called "Jacobean" book-plates. In this style the device is displayed either on a shield, or on a circular or oval panel, enclosed in an ornamental framed cartouche. Characteristic of this form is the "lining" of the framework which acts as a background for the arms. Its treatment, known as "imbrication," consists of crossed diagonal lines in the work of Hurd (Plate 19) and Syng; the overlapping wavy lines resembling fish scales, that John Burt used; or the simulated brickwork found on pieces by Potwine and Blowers. The silversmith often introduced into the lining, below or above the arms, grotesque faces or a scallop shell. The evenly balanced scrolled frame of the cartouche offered suitable space for the introduction of lions, eagles, pots of fruit and flowers, and even human figures.

The harmonious proportion and balance displayed between plain and decorated surfaces together with the technical excellence of its cast and engraved ornament attest to the high standard of workmanship maintained by the American silversmith, whose work while reflecting European styles has a distinct flavor of its own, the product of its locale and age.

Plate 21

a) *The popularity of the monteith in the Colonies as late as 1773 is exemplified by this bowl fashioned by Daniel Henchman and engraved by his brother-in-law, Nathaniel Hurd. Diameter* $10\frac{3}{4}''$

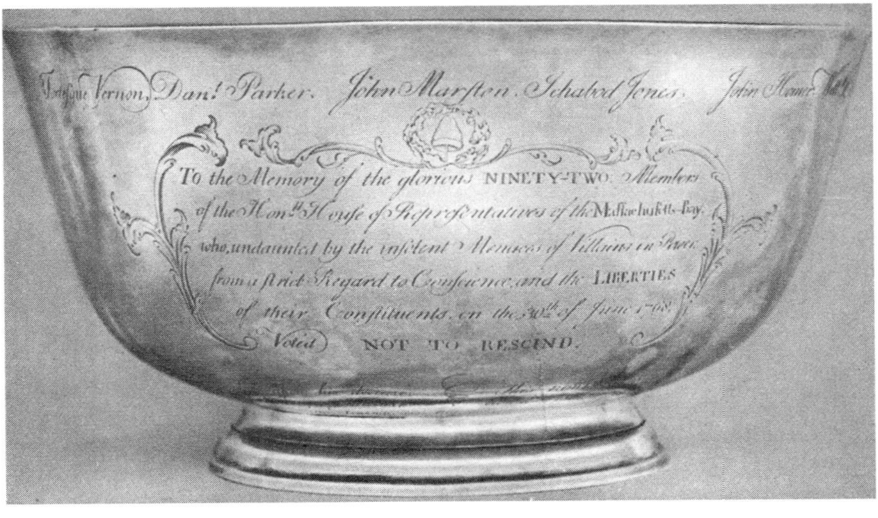

b) *Paul Revere fashioned in 1768, for fifteen fellow members of the Sons of Liberty, this bowl celebrating the defiance by the Massachusetts House of Representatives of George III on the eve of the American Revolution. Diameter 11″*

Plate 22

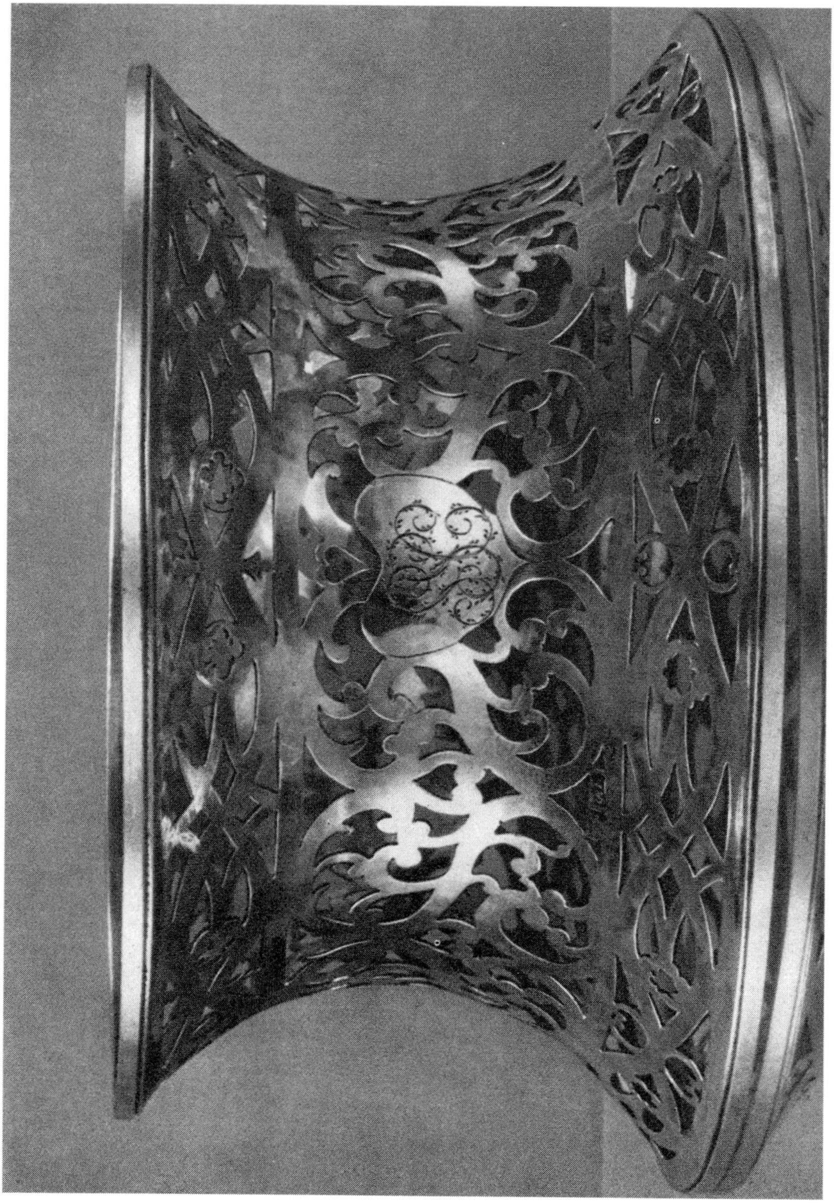

The unique dish ring by Myer Myers displays the craftsman's imaginative treatment in its intricate interlaced design of geometric, Rococo and Gothic ornament. Diameter, base, 8 $\frac{15}{16}$"

BANCKER

Chapter five

The Exuberance of the Rococo, 1750-1785

BY THE LATE 1730'S, SOCIETY'S EVER-PRESENT DESIRE FOR NOVELTY ushered into London a new mode which spread like wildfire to furniture, china, dress and all forms of the decorative arts. In silver the plain shapes associated with the Queen Anne style were gradually discarded for those based upon the rococo mode, then popular in northwestern Europe, and noticeably in France, seat of its origin. The style was based upon the use of asymmetrical forms, sinuous S- and C- shaped curves, and restless rocaille ornament composed of fantastic rockwork, shell, scrolls, leaf and floral patterns expressed in engraved, chased, pierced or cast forms. Its chief shortcoming lay in its tendency to extravagant design and the sacrifice of shape to ornament with the resultant effect of instability.

The style made its appearance in the colonies following the successful ending of King George's War (1748) and the country's return to conditions favorable to trade. At the time it was adopted, the style was but a modification of the London mode and was chiefly expressed in the use of pear- and inverted pear-shaped forms, double scrolled handles, cast shell and C-scroll ornament, and, in its most artistic form, the rendering of beautifully engraved and skillfully pierced rocaille designs.

Closer political relations with England brought about by a common objective during the French and Indian Wars (1756–1763) helped to make the colonies conscious of the changing London modes; they expressed this in the use of richer architectural ornament, drawn from English publications, in their mansions, and in furniture from the fashionable designs of Thomas Chippendale. The ever-increasing importation of English silver for the masses, apparent after 1758, as opposed to the individual orders of rich merchants in the preceding period, supplied the models for this new fashion. Newspapers of the period abound in long advertisements of these imports. Both Zachariah Brigden and Daniel Parker were steady advertisers in the Boston papers of the 1760's, offering imported silver, jewelry, raw materials and all sorts of silversmith's tools. Similar offers are found in the papers of New York, Philadelphia and Charleston; in the latter city, in 1765, John Paul Grimké advertises "Sterling plate imported from London."

The variety of forms in vogue is indicated by the advertisement appearing in the *Boston News Letter* of Jan. 9, 1772: "Cox & Berry, at their Store near the British Coffee House in King Street, have just Imported in the last Ships from London, a great Variety of Articles, including Plate, as Tankards, Coffee-Pots, Cans, Waiters, Frames and Casters, Cream Ewers and Urns, Salts, Wine Funnels, Sauce Boats & Ladles, Tureen Ladles, Table and Tea Spoon, Salt Ladles and Shovels, Punch Ladles, silver gilt plain and chas'd Corrals, Spring Tea Tongs, Decanter Labels, Decanter Corks with Silver Tops, Silver Thimbles, Nutmeg Graters; a great variety of Silver Buckles, Silver-mounted Swords and Hangers, Etwee and Pencil Cases, Silver, Snake and Jack Watch Chains, Scissor Chains, Silver-mounted Snuff Boxes, Gold Stock Buckles" as well as a long list of plated articles. In November of the same year "Roberts & Lee, Jewellers, opposite the old Brick Meeting House in Cornhill," stated in their advertisement that "Town and Country Goldsmiths may be supplied with every article usually imported . . . on very advantageous terms." In the face of such competition the colonial craftsman had to maintain high standards and give his imagination full play to ensure his economic survival. The resentment of local craftsmen against this competition is eloquently expressed by Roberts & Lee's neighbour, Daniel Henchman, in the *Boston Evening Post* of Jan. 18, 1773:

DANIEL HENCHMAN

Takes this Method to inform his Customers in Town and Country, that he still continues to carry on the GOLD and SILVERSMITHS Business at his shop opposite the Old Brick Meeting House in Cornhill, where he makes with his own Hands all Kinds of large and small Plate Work in the genteelest Taste and newest Fashion, and of the purest Silver; and as his work has hitherto met with the Approbation of the most curious, he flatters himself that he shall have the Preference by Those who are Judges of Work, to those Strangers among us who import and sell English Plate, to the great Hurt and Prejudice of the Towns-men who have been bred to the Business.

—Said HENCHMAN therefore will engage to those Gentlemen and Ladies who shall please to employ him, that he will make any kind of Plate they may want equal in Goodness and cheaper than any they can import from London, with the greatest Dispatch."

Little change is noticed in the usual forms of ecclesiastical plate other than the addition of pear-shaped canns for communion vessels and a greater emphasis in general on the use of curved lines, together with beautifully executed engraved arms of the donors within a rocaille surround of leaf and floral pattern. Based on a traditional style and exotic by contrast with the prim vessels of the Protestant Church are the florid ornaments fashioned about 1765 by Myer Myers (1723–1795) for the newly designed Synagogue by Peter Harrison at Newport. Known as Crowns of the Law and used as ornaments for the wooden rollers around which is rolled the Pentateuch, they exhibit in their richly executed pierced, chased and engraved decoration of scrolled acanthus leaves, flowers and gilt bells, the contemporary expression of another culture which was finding a haven on these shores.

Of the domestic plate, the flatware offers a large variety of pattern and form. Table, tea, soup, and salt spoons follow the earlier form with a small "v" in the center of the up-curved handle tip. The Queen Anne baroque shell ornament on the back of the bowl is replaced by the florid rococo shell. By 1770, the handle tip becomes more rounded, turns down; the edges are decorated with a chased border of short oblique lines, known as "feather edge" (Plate 2b). The accompanying patterns stamped on the back of the bowl include floral forms and a bird sitting on top of an open cage along with the motto "I Love Liberty." Some large spoons and ladles made in New York and Philadelphia show the adoption of the

English Onslow pattern, in which the cast handle is treated as an Ionic volute, with a series of deeply cut lines converging to a point part-way down the spoon and with a fluted bowl for ladles. Such spoons are listed in a Philadelphia advertisement of 1763 as "fluted and polished sauce spoons, with scroll heads." The fork, which was still rare, follows the spoon fashions. The arms of the scissor-type sugar tongs employ more curves and terminate in shell grips, until the 1760's, when the bow-shaped spring tongs appear. The cast and chased arms, pierced in intricate rococo designs, terminating in shell grips, are joined by a hammered arched spring back, hence the contemporary term "spring tongs." Knives, largely imported, were of the pistol-handle variety.

The porringer is universally found with the pierced scrolled "keyhole" handle, with the addition in New York of an interlacing pattern featuring a central lozenge (Page 109), a characteristic detail of the New York chair-back in the Chippendale style. Current furniture styles are also reflected in the shell edge decorating the rims of circular salts as well as in their supporting shell and claw feet. Late in the period one finds salts with oval bodies similarly decorated as well as the straight thin-walled salts, pierced in geometric design, with glass liners, whose English models were advertised in Philadelphia by 1770.

Casters having a pear- and inverted pear-shaped body on moulded foot with a tall pierced domed cover surmounted by a flame finial are found. The sauceboat, still boat-shaped, with serrated or beaded rim, has a much narrower lip and body, resting on three bandy or cabriole legs with cast shell ornaments at the knee and foot. The double-scrolled handle is frequently decorated with the functional acanthus-leaf purchase. Later in the period, the bandy legs were discarded for an oval gadrooned foot supporting a boat-shaped body decorated with a gadrooned band along the simple curving lip, as on three fashioned by Paul Revere (Museum of Fine Arts).

The tankard, which retained its popularity, shows in Boston a slightly more tapering body frequently encircled by a mid-band, with the domed cover topped by a twisted flame finial, similar in form to those employed on contemporary highboys and secretary-bookcases. The rococo

Plate 23

The silversmith's use of the popular inverted pear shape, as well as his exploitation of the aesthetic possibilities of asymmetry, is expressed in the cast, flat-chased and engraved ornament of the tea kettle and stand made by the Quaker silversmith Joseph Richardson, Sr., prior to 1760. Height 14½"

a) *The elongated pear-shaped body, flame finial, gadrooned foot and shell ornament on the spout of this coffee pot by Revere are typical of the Rococo style. Height* $11\frac{1}{4}''$

b) *Inkstand in the Rococo manner fashioned by Philip Syng in 1752 at a cost of £25 16s. for the Pennsylvania Assembly. It was used by the Signers of the Declaration of Independence and of the Constitution. Length* $10\frac{1}{4}''$

influence in all localities is expressed in a freer use of the reverse curve evidenced in the pear-shaped body, similar to the cann, with domed cover and open pierced thumbpiece, resting on a moulded and splayed base. The double handle often ends in an ornate shield or scrolled tip. One also finds in New York a continuance of the flat-topped tankard, and one by Richard van Dyck (1715–1770) made early in the period combines the conventional features with flat-chased ornament on its cover (Garvan Collection). Many of these flat-topped tankards have pierced thumbpieces, resembling the New York chair-back of Gothic inspiration. An example now in the Garvan Collection was fashioned by Capt. Elias Pelletreau (1726–1810) of Long Island in 1772 for Hugh Smith. According to Pelletreau's daybook (now in the possession of the Long Island Historical Society), Smith was charged as follows:

3pt. tankard	35 oz. 7 dwt. at 9s. 6d.	£16	10	10
Fashioning		4	8	8
Engraving cypher			6	0
		£21	5	6

Since at this time a day laborer was paid at the rate of 3 Yorkshire shillings per day, such an investment represented the wages for more than four and a half months. That the silversmith was not always paid in cash, or plate, but by services rendered, or goods in exchange, is borne out by the following bill with its curious book-keeping preserved in the Frost family papers (George S. Frost Estate):

1774	Capt. George Frost to Wm. Cario		Dr.	
Novr.	9 towards a pr. of Silver Buckels	4	12	0
	for making a 1/2 Doz. of Tea Spoons	9	0	0
		£13	0	0
Cr.	by 2 quarters of lamb	3	12	0
	by Silver left	1	16	0
		5	8	0
By Cash in full				

William Cario.

Punch was still greatly esteemed, even enlivening college commencements, judging from a surviving monteith associated with the founding of Dartmouth College. It is an interesting example of the late survival in America of this form, which had become obsolete in England in the days of Queen Anne. Its plain hemispherical bowl (Plate 21a) resting on a moulded and splayed foot is capped by a detachable rim, ornamented with cast scrolled borders. It was fashioned by Daniel Henchman, whose newspaper advertisement was quoted earlier in this chapter. Henchman's brother-in-law, Nathaniel Hurd, engraved and signed on its side the legend:

His Excellency John Wentworth Esq./Governor of the Province of New Hampshire/ And those Friends who accompanied him/To Dartmouth College the first Commencement 1771/In Testimony of their Gratitude and Good Wishes/Present this to the Rev[d.] Eleazer Wheelock, D.D. President/And to his Successors in that Office.

The shape of the punch bowl generally favored in Boston had a plain body with an everted lip on a moulded splayed foot as shown on one made in 1763 by William Homes. It was

The Gift/of the Field Officers and/Captains of the Regiment/of the Town of Boston to/ Thomas Dawes Esq[r.] for his past Services as Ad/jutant to said Re-/giment Sept 13/1763. [Museum of Fine Arts.]

Of a similar shape is the more famous one fashioned in 1768 by Paul Revere, popularly known today as "The Sons of Liberty Bowl" (Plate 21b). Its origin and appearance were thus described in the *Boston Gazette*, August 8, 1768:

We hear that the Week before last was finished by Order and for the Use of the Gentlemen belonging to the Insurance Office kept by Mr. *Nathaniel Barber*, at the North-End, an elegant Silver BOWL, weighing *forty-five* ounces, and holding *forty-five* Jills. On one side is engraved within a handsome Border—*To the Memory of the Glorious* NINETY-TWO *Members of the Honourable House of the* REPRESENTATIVES *of the* MASSACHUSETTS-BAY, *who undaunted by the insolent Menaces of Villains in Power, and out of a strict Regard to Conscience, and the* LIBERTIES *of their Constituents, on the 30th of June 1768,* VOTED NOT TO RESCIND. *Over which is the Cap of Liberty in an Oaken Crown. On the other Side, in a Circle adorned with Flowers, etc. is No. 45.* WILKES AND LIBERTY, *under which is General Warrants torn to Pieces. On the Top of the Cap of Liberty, and out of each Side, is a Standard, on one is* MAGNA CHARTA, *the other* BILL OF RIGHTS.

—On Monday Evening last, the Gentlemen belonging to the Office made a Genteel Entertainment, and invited a Number of Gentlemen of Distinction in the Town, when 45 Loyal Toasts were drank, and the whole concluded with a new Song, the Chorus of which is, *In Freedom we're born, and in Freedom we'll live,* etc.

To the Bostonian of 1768, the symbolism would have been quite clear, but in 1949 an explanation is required. John Wilkes, English agitator and reformer, had in the 45th issue of his paper—*The North Briton*—in 1763 attacked the royal policy of suppressing colonial self-government. As a result of this article King George III issued a general warrant on which Wilkes was imprisoned, his house searched and papers seized. Wilkes, elected to Parliament in 1768, became a popular hero in Boston, where "No. 45" became a patriotic slogan. In 1768 the Massachusetts House of Representatives protested to the King against such repressive trade measures as the Townshend Acts and at the same time sent letters to the other American colonies urging a united front. This letter they were ordered to rescind but, as the bowl's inscription tells us, by a vote of 92 to 17 they defied the royal order. "No. 45" and "The Illustrious Ninety-two" became popular toasts at all patriotic gatherings. A similar spirit is expressed a little later in a different way in New York where three days after the Battle of Bunker's Hill, Charles Oliver Bruff offers: "Those Gentlemen who are forming Themselves into Companies in Defense of their Liberties, and others that are not provided with Swords, may be suited therewith by applying to Charles Oliver Bruff in Maiden-Lane, near the Fly-Market. Small Swords Silver mounted, Cut-and-thrust and Cutteau De Chase, mounted with beautiful Green grips; and Broad Swords with the Heads of Lord Chatham, and John Wilkes, Esq.; with Shells pierced and ornamented with Mottoes—for Pitt's Head, Magna Charta and Freedom,—for Wilkes's Head, Wilkes and Liberty..." (The *New York Gazette* and *The Weekly Mercury,* June 19, 1775).

The favorite punch-bowl shape in New York was a footed bowl whose broad curved body was enriched by fine heraldic engraving, as on one fashioned by John Heath for the Van Cortlandt family, or decorated with flat-chased ornament, composed of reticulated diapered reserves, shells, scrolls and flowers, as on two surviving examples by Richard van Dyck.

Of the accessories necessary to the punch bowl, the lemon strainer, with its two scrolled handles and pierced circular shallow bowl sometimes edged with a gadrooned band, offered an opportunity for imaginative treatment by the silversmith. One fashioned in 1765, the year of the passage of the Stamp Act, by Jonathan Clarke of Newport and Providence, is of particular interest in that it bears perforated in the bowl the following inscription: "JABEZ BOWEN PROVIDENCE JANUARY 1765" encircling a central petal design. Even more intricate in its piercing is the dish ring or support for silver or china bowls and hot dishes as a protection for the highly polished tables. Although there are numerous references to them in the advertisements of imported plate, they are today among the rarities of English and American silver. The unique American example in the Garvan Collection (Plate 22) was fashioned by Myer Myers for the Hon. Samuel Cornell, a wealthy New York merchant with holdings in North Carolina, where he had served as a member of His Majesty's Council prior to the Revolution. Reel-shaped with concave body, strengthened by heavy mouldings at top and bottom, it is pierced by an intricate pattern of leafy scrolls and hearts, banded with borders of interlacing strap work, quatrefoils and lozenges. It displays the brilliant craftsmanship of Myers, who had become chairman of the New York Gold and Silversmiths' Society in 1786. While in general shape it is close to those rings popular in eighteenth-century Ireland, which in recent years have been erroneously termed "potato rings," the pierced pattern by Myers is distinctly American in conception as well as execution. The same maker's decanter-stands, now in the New York Historical Society, display a similar design in their pierced sides.

Social life centered around the walnut or mahogany tea table, which cabinetmakers versed in the rococo mode skillfully enriched with elaborately carved pedestal and with ball and claw feet and pie-crust rim. In 1759 Ezra Stiles estimated that of the 1,940 families on Cape Cod "1500 drink Tea which may drink 1000^{lb} Tea per annum 1000 Dollars, or £250 Ster . . . Boston $16{,}000^{lb}$ Tea." The earliest rococo form of

Plate 25

a) *Montreal Medal, 1760, by Daniel Christian Fueter, made for presentation to the leading Indian chieftains who aided the British in the conquest of Montreal during the French and Indian wars. Diameter* $1\frac{3}{4}''$

b) *Bookplates in the Chippendale style as interpreted by Paul Revere and Nathaniel Hurd*

Plate 26

Benjamin Burt's tankard of 1786 is decorated in the typical bright-cut ornament, based upon Adam design. Height 9⅛"

teapot was of bullet shape, a development from the Queen Anne globular form. This in turn was succeeded by an inverted pear-shaped body with stepped foot and a domed cover surmounted by a cast finial, with single or double scrolled wooden handle. A flat-chased rococo decoration on the shoulder was used on one pot made in Boston by Thomas Edwards, who died in 1755. "Chased silver teapots, newest fashion" were still being advertised in 1759. As shown in the realistic portrayal (see frontispiece) by his friend and patron, John Singleton Copley, Paul Revere holds in his hand a plain version of this type resting on a sand pillow, with the engraving and chasing tools on a work table near by (Museum of Fine Arts).

For chasing the pot was filled with pitch against which the design could be hammered with the piece cushioned on the sand pillow. An inverted pear-shaped teapot with chased ornament is in the Thayer Collection of the Museum of Fine Arts. The larger number of those fashioned in Boston and Philadelphia have a simplicity of surface, enriched only by the owner's engraved arms or cypher. The New York type on the other hand is invariably chased, but the craftsman strikes an excellent balance between ornament and shape, and none of the known American examples are guilty of the over-ornamentation of their London contemporaries.

Two examples of the inverted pear-shaped form are supported on three cast bandy legs and feet, a treatment also found on the sugar basin and cream jug. The long period of popularity enjoyed by the inverted pear form is due to the fact that little silver was made during the Revolutionary War. Revere's biographical statement relative to the period in which he made his famous ride, immortalized by Longfellow, is quite pertinent here: "My father was a Goldsmith . . . I learned the trade of him & have carried on the business ever since; until the year 1775 when the American Revolution began; from that time till May 1780, I have been in the Government service as Lieut. Col. of an Artillery regiment."

The first reaction against the curves of the rococo is indicated in 1782 by the introduction of the cylindrical drum-shaped teapot with gadrooned or beaded edges, straight spout, domed cover and cast pine-cone finial.

Such a one, fashioned in 1783 by Revere for Moses Michael Hayes, is recorded in his ledger.

Mr. M. M. Hayes Dr.	
To a silver Teapot wt 16: 14 @ 7/	£5 16 10
Making £4.16. Handle 6/ engraving cypher 12/	5 14 0
To a silver Cream pot w. 5.10 @ 7/	1 18 6
Making 42/ engraving cypher 6/	2 8 0
Excise on 22 oz.—4 silver @ 6d pr. oz.	0 11 5
	£16 8 9

The linear emphasis expressed in this teapot bears the same relation to the inverted pear-shaped form as the Marlborough (straight) leg in furniture does to the cabriole, and anticipates the style which follows.

The cream pot made to accompany the Hayes teapot (both in the Bortman Collection) retains the inverted pear-shaped form that had replaced the earlier pear-shaped cream jug inherited from the Queen Anne period; but the cream pot is treated with flat-chased or engraved rocaille ornament and the pad foot is supplanted by shell or ball and claw forms borrowed from the chair foot. One transitional shape, illustrating a combination of the inverted pear-shape with bandy legs, is ludicrous. It is unfortunate that none of the "silver cows" advertised in 1773 by William Whetcroft of Annapolis has survived to show an American interpretation of a form popular in contemporary England in both silver and ceramics.

The sugar basin in Boston follows the same general form as the teapot, its domed and moulded cover often surmounted by the same twisted flame finial as the tankard, varied sometimes by a cast floral ornament. Two examples are known of inverted pear-shaped bodies with reel-shaped handles on their domed covers, supported by cast legs terminating in toed or hoofed feet. The New Yorker favored a somewhat larger inverted pear form with cast finial or reel-shaped handle treated to simulate the edge of a shell. The Philadelphia form invariably employs a flame finial with a gadrooned or feathered edge on the everted lip of the basin.

Mrs. Benjamin Franklin, writing in 1765 to her husband, then in London, desires him to "remember a pair of silver canisters" and notes with some satisfaction that there is among the furnishings of the blue room "a very handsome stand for the tea kettle to stand on, and the ornamental china." Yet only one tea kettle and stand has survived, a handsome example by Joseph Richardson, Sr., fashioned for the rich widow of a Philadelphia mayor, and mentioned in her will of 1755. Richardson's sense of proportion and manipulative skill is demonstrated in his balanced use of design and ornament composed of repoussé, flat-chased, cast and engraved rocaille detail (Plate 23). Although it is one of the most ornate pieces made in Philadelphia, one is struck by its restraint, when it is compared with those fashioned by Paul de Lamerie in London in 1751.

By the middle of the eighteenth century, the fashionable London coffee pot had a pear-shaped body with low splayed foot, a narrow neck, moulded domed cover with a finely cast finial, cast shell-decorated spout and scrolled wooden handle. Such a coffee pot, dated 1751, was ordered from London by Peter Faneuil's heir, Benjamin Faneuil, and might have served as a model for those made early in the period by Daniel Henchman, Nathaniel Hurd, Samuel Minott and Paul Revere. The latter craftsman varied the usual form by enriching the foot and cover edge with a chased gadrooned moulding, employing a flame finial on the cover. That this style persisted for some years is evidenced by the coffee pot that Revere fashioned for Commodore John Paul Jones under the following romantic circumstances. In 1778 when Scottish-born Jones raided the coast of Scotland his men carried off the ancient family plate of the Earl of Selkirk, which was sold in France in May 1778 for prize money. Jones purchased the plate and returned it to the Countess of Selkirk with a letter in which he declared: "Though I have drawn my sword in the present generous struggle for the rights of men, yet I am not in arms merely as an American, nor am I in pursuit of riches . . . I profess myself a citizen of the world, totally unfettered by the little mean distinctions of climate, or country, which diminish the benevolence of the heart and set bounds to philanthropy." The Earl's gratitude to Jones was memorialized in this coffee pot (Plate 24a) bearing on its side the arms and motto of the "Father of the American Navy" (Collection of Mr. and Mrs. Walter M. Jeffords). Of equal charm and rarity is a finely proportioned pear-shaped pot with rounded bottom supported by three spreading finely cast shell feet, fashioned by Revere for Richard Derby in 1772. Contemporary with the pear-shaped form was the inverted pear or "chased and plain double and single belly'd coffee-pots" as they are aptly termed in Edmond Milne's advertisement in the *Pennsylvania Journal* of Dec. 15, 1763. This form was popular in all localities and persisted as late as 1791.

Large- and small-footed salvers or "waiters" follow the same decorative pattern as the contemporary tea tables in their charming applied cast moulded rims, ornamented with C-scrolls, shells and gadrooning supported on cast shell, claw, or ball and claw feet. With finely engraved rocaille arms they rank artistically among the finest pieces of the period as attested by the surviving examples of Thomas Edwards and Paul Revere, Boston; Lewis Fueter, Thomas Hammersley, Myer Myers and George Ridout, New York; Joseph Richardson, Sr., and Philip Syng, Jr., Philadelphia.

Cast and chased candlesticks, square in section, with baluster stem, moulded base, square nozzle are decorated with corded bands, mouldings and shell ornament emphasizing the corners of foot and nozzle. Accompanying snuffer trays, rectangular in shape, with cast and chased high scrolled handle, cast shaped borders of C-scrolls and shell motif, are supported on four cast shell or scroll feet. Examples by Myer Myers and Philip Syng, Jr., are known. And although "silver pillar'd and fluted candlesticks of the corinthian order" are advertised among importations by Edmund Milne in 1764, only one pair by Joseph and Nathaniel Richardson have come to the writer's attention. A pair of chamber sticks having low sockets resting in a deep saucer, with gadrooned edge and ring-shaped handle by Myer Myers is privately owned.

One of the pieces richest in historical associations is the inkstand (Plate 24b) fashioned in 1752 by Philip Syng, Jr., for the Pennsylvania Assembly at a cost of £25 16s. The rocaille decoration of its shaped tray

Plate 27

a) *1787 punch bowl by Revere, showing in both form and decoration the influence of the newly imported Chinese export porcelain bowls. Diameter* $9\frac{1}{4}''$

b) *One of the latest shapes popularized by Revere was his adaptation of the Liverpool jug, in which form follows function. Height* $6\frac{1}{8}''$

Characteristic of the classical style, peculiar to Philadelphia, was the use of the pierced gallery as well as the fine beaded mouldings, as in this tea set fashioned by Abraham Dubois. Height, teapot, $11\frac{1}{4}''$

and feet is similar to that of the salvers, and its containers for sand, ink, and quill pens follow closely the contemporary English pattern. It was used in 1776 by the Signers of the Declaration of Independence and again in 1787 by the representatives of those colonies adopting the Constitution. Today it is appropriately housed in Independence Hall.

Among the smaller items fashioned by the silversmith are the shaped and chased snuff-boxes, chased shell-edged shoe, knee and stock buckles in both silver and gold, as well as the charming oval lockets and octagonal sleeve buttons of gold with richly engraved surface. One of the outstanding pieces of craftsmanship in gold is a rocaille, chased whistle and bells with coral, bearing the stamp of Daniel Christian Fueter (Plate III). It was a fond grandmother's gift to her eldest grand-daughter and namesake. One wonders whether the chasing was not the work of the skilled John Anthony Beau, since in July 1769 Fueter "informs the Public that Mr. John Anthony Beau, Chaiser, from Geneva works with him; where chaising in general viz. Snuff Boxes, Watch Cases, &c. &c. is done in the best and cheapest Manner." Fueter is best remembered as the maker of two sets of medals presented by Sir William Johnson, sole agent and superintendent of the Six Nations and all other Indians inhabiting British territory north of the Ohio River and the Carolinas, with appropriate ceremony, to high-ranking Indian Chiefs. The earlier medal, a circular piece dating from 1760 and bearing a flat-chased city view with the legend "MONTREAL," was presented to the chieftains of the several hundred Indians who participated in the successful expedition against Montreal during the French and Indian Wars (Plate 25a). The other, presented in 1764 to those chiefs pledging British alliance following the crushing defeat of Pontiac's conspiracy, carries on the obverse a bust portrait in relief of King George III and on the reverse a scene in relief of a pipe-bearing Indian sitting under a peace tree in friendly conversation with an Englishman, along with the legend, "HAPPY WHILE UNITED, 1764." Earlier than these is a gorget bearing the mark of Joseph Richardson, Sr., on which is engraved a Sun in splendor with an Indian seated by a fire and about to receive a peace pipe from an Englishman sitting under the shade of the peace tree; it is believed to have been made for

"The Friendly Association for regaining and preserving Peace with the Indians by Pacific Measures," of which society Richardson was a member (Historical Society of Pennsylvania).

One of the most engaging aspects of the rococo silver is the delightful rocaille heraldic engraving in which the coat-of-arms is displayed in an asymmetrical cartouche of pear or shell shape, surrounded by shell ornament enriched with an airy, playful pattern of C-scrolls and delicate sprays of realistic leaves and flowers. The engraving bears an even closer relation to the contemporary bookplate than in the preceding period. Many of the silversmiths were adept at both, the two best-known being Paul Revere and Nathaniel Hurd (Plates 25b and c). In the portrait by Copley (Cleveland Museum of Art, Plate IV) the latter is shown with two books, the larger lettered in red, "Display of Heraldry/J.Guillim." This was a standard book of heraldry in the eighteenth century and undoubtedly the source of many of the heraldic devices engraved on colonial silver. In the expression of the rocaille decoration, however, one discerns the subtlety and imagination of the silversmith. And while there are numerous advertisements in the newspapers of the period of London engravers who are ready to engrave coats-of-arms, cyphers and other devices on plate, nevertheless surviving bills by John Heath, Nathaniel Hurd and Paul Revere bear evidence that the arms on their pieces are their own handiwork, the product of their own times, expressing with grace and delicacy the American version of the flowery spirit of Thomas Chippendale, whose name today popularly serves to describe his age.

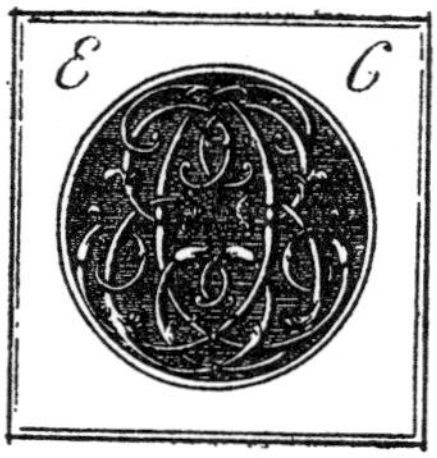

The cypher E C from S. Sympson's A New Book of Cyphers, *London, c. 1726*

MYERS

Chapter six

The Classical Reserve of the Federal Style, 1785-1810

THE SAME DESIRE FOR NOVELTY THAT HAD POPULARIZED THE rococo mode in the second quarter of the eighteenth century caused its discard in the third, when the fresh excavations at Pompeii and Herculaneum began to fascinate a world brought up on the Latin poets. The recapture of the past, and in particular the details of domestic life, in an age when moralists were patterning the perfect society on the ancient republics of Greece and Rome, provided a new inspirational source for the decorative arts. In England, the brothers Adam were the chief interpreters of the classical style in which emphasis was placed on straight structural lines or unbroken curves and delicate pencil lines of inlay, as expressed, for example, in the furniture designs of Hepplewhite and Sheraton.

The extreme simplicity of form and precise proportion of this classically inspired style appealed to the new republic, whose national motto, decimal currency, form of federal government, as well as public architecture, were all based on Roman forms. In silver as in furniture, the style is chiefly exemplified in straight structural lines, emphasized by delicately engraved parallel bands of bright-cut ornament, beaded or reeded mouldings, ovoid and elliptical shapes, both plain and fluted and urn-shaped finials. The popularity of the urn shape is demonstrated in its selection as a symbol by the Philadelphia Goldsmiths and Silversmiths. In the federal procession of July 4, 1788, celebrating the Declaration of Independence and the establishment of the Constitution, the representatives of these crafts carried a silk flag portraying the Genius of America holding in her hand a silver urn, with the following motto: "The purity, brightness and solidity of this metal is emblematical of that Liberty which we expect from the new Constitution."

The source of the silver forms is to be found in the English imports, for although we had achieved political independence, culturally and artistically we were as dependent upon the mother country as before the war. In 1790 Joseph Anthony, Jr., was advertising in Philadelphia, then the seat of the Federal Government, silver of "entire new patterns," and a decade later another craftsman, James Musgrave, promised that "sets of plate of any pattern if ordered will be executed at the shortest notice. He has on hand a large assortment of silverware, such as coffee and tea pots, sugar bowls, milk pots and slop bowls in sets or separate, fluted and plain." (*Pennsylvania Packet,* Nov. 6, 1800.)

This new style is evidenced in ecclesiastical plate by a beaker with body of ovoid shape resting on a low moulded foot, as in one by Revere in 1795; or of goblet shape, with a high trumpet foot, with beaded edge, as fashioned by Miles Gorham in 1804 for the First Congregational Church, Derby, Conn. Three graceful two-handled covered cups made originally for the Brattle Street Church by Joseph Loring epitomize the style with their use of an ovoid body, trumpet foot, tall domical incurved cover, surmounted by an urn-shaped finial, angular handles, and horizontal reeded mouldings on body and foot of cup. The inscription in Roman letters is engraved within a bright-cut oval medallion on the front.

Of domestic plate, the spoon is still the most common article found in all sizes. During the period 1785–1800, it has a pointed bowl and down-turned handle, often plain, except for a script monogram, and is similar to contemporary Scottish silver; a popular form of ornament known as bright-cut consisting of a delicate shallow engraved or chased pattern of zigzag lines is often found decorating the handle edge or forming an oval medallion for the monogram on the handle (Plate 2b). The backs of the spoon bowls are often decorated in relief with a variety of patterns ranging from a plain rounded, or "heel," drop or an acanthus leaf, to a long-tailed dove holding an olive branch in its beak, particularly popular among the Quaker clients of Philadelphia and Wilmington and confined (with one exception in New York) to those localities.

Another decoration, popular in the inlays of furniture and as signs for inns, following the adoption of the U.S. Seal, is the American eagle, which has been found on the backs of Philadelphia spoon bowls and undoubtedly dates from the days when that city was the nation's capital. A slight variant in the handle has two small, spur-like projections at the jointure of the bowl, used by Revere as early as 1787. By 1800, the mania for funeral display, heightened by the universal mourning for Washington, popularized in New England and New York a spoon whose squared-end handle is clipped at the corner to simulate a coffin, and is hence designated "coffin-end" (Plate 2b). They are found completely plain or decorated with a restrained bright-cut reserve for the monogram. Tablespoons, teaspoons, salt, mustard and dessert spoons, ladles and forks of the period follow the same general pattern. Bow-shaped sugar tongs had come to be made in one piece, with solid arms, plain or engraved, ending in oval or acorn grips.

The porringer is still found with the "keyhole" handle, in which the scrolls of the piercing are more delicate than the robust ones of earlier periods. The appearance in New York of a fan-shaped handle by Hugh Wishart offers a novel variation (Page 127). Closely associated in use, is the small pap-boat for infant feeding. Inspired by the Roman lamp, its functional plain boat-shaped body with a long everted lip is occasionally decorated with a beaded moulding.

The tankard lost its popularity in this period which was plagued by the beginnings of the temperance movement. The form in Boston differs little from the earlier tankard other than in its engraved decoration. One such tankard (Plate 26) was fashioned by Benjamin Burt in 1786 as a worthy commemoration of the construction of the Charles River Bridge, which, according to the *Travels in New England and New York* (1821) of Yale's President, the Rev. Timothy Dwight, "was the first effort to erect a bridge over a broad river in the American states . . . and is one thousand five hundred and three feet in length—the river being here two hundred and eighty feet wider than the Thames at Westminster Bridge. About forty large bridges have been built in the United States in consequence of this structure." Engraved above the mid-band are two equidistant oval panels connected by floral garlands in the bright-cut manner, one containing a view of the bridge, the other the legend:

Presented to/Richard Devens, Esqr:/by the Proprietors of/Charles River Bridge,/in Testimony of their entire Approbation/of his faithful Services,/as a Special Director of that Work/begun A.D. 1785/and perfected/A.D.1786. [M. & M. Karolik Collection, Museum of Fine Arts.]

Another director, Capt. David Wood, received a teapot similarly engraved by Zachariah Brigden. Toward the end of the eighteenth century cylindrical tankards, with flat covers and pierced thumbpieces, are found in New York and Philadelphia. By 1800, examples of this shape with hooped bands, barrel-fashion, are universally found in which all sense of proportion seems to have been lost. Mugs follow the general tankard shapes and decoration. The cann continues with a slightly more elongated body, the foot decorated by a beaded moulding, with the engraved ornament in the fashionable bright-cut manner. The ovoid-shaped goblet with trumpet foot, and the flat-bottomed tumbler with plain or panelled sides are found in sets, both plain and engraved.

The establishment of American free trade in the European and Asiatic ports following the Revolution is responsible for an increased influence of ceramic shapes on the silver of the period. An interesting comparison may be made between a porcelain bowl painted at Canton in 1786 for Elias Hasket Derby and brought to Salem in that year (Peabody Institute Museum, Salem), and a silver punch bowl (Plate 27a) fashioned in 1787 by Revere (Garvan Collection). The shape and foot are identical. The delicate painted decoration of the rim of the porcelain bowl is executed by Revere in a graceful bright-cut pattern. On one side within a floral garland is the script monogram W.S. and on the other the legend:

To/GENERAL WILLIAM SHEPARD/Presented by/The MILITIA of Springfield/As a Memorial of his Ability/and Zeal in quelling/SHAYS'S REBELLION/at/Springfield Arsenal/January 25th 1787.

Plate 29

Revere's urn of 1800 with its ovoid body, incurved conical cover, urn finial, loop handles, as well as the ornamental features, is typical of the classical style at its peak. Height 19"

Plate 30

Indian Peace Medal of 1793 by Joseph Richardson, Jr., showing obverse and reverse. Height $5\frac{5}{16}$"

This recalls vividly the post-Revolutionary depression during which currency deflation and high taxes caused an epidemic of mortgage foreclosures, embittering the farmers of western Massachusetts to such an extent that open rebellion broke out. It is thought that as a result of the alarm caused by Shays's Rebellion Massachusetts became disposed to ratify the Federal Constitution two weeks later.

Another ceramic shape exploited by Revere was the Liverpool jug, which reached the height of its popularity around 1800 as a favorite form of Washington memorial. Its barrel-shaped body, slightly flared at foot and rim, has a triangular spout and simple scroll handle (Plate 27b). Of the several surviving examples, including two made for the use of Revere's family, the only dated example is that presented in 1804 by the parishioners of the First Church in Milton to their retiring pastor (Collection, Henry F. du Pont). This shape, while one of Revere's latest, is also one of his most functional, combining as it does extreme simplicity of form and a precision of proportion intelligible to all.

The sideboard, a new piece of dining-room furniture, encouraged the making of matching tea services which by 1800 were sufficiently common to be advertised in the Philadelphia daily papers. The display of an elaborate tea equipage in use in Connecticut's provincial capital impressed an even more provincial lady, Mrs. Anstis Lee, who comments thus in her *Narrative of a Horseback Journey to Connecticut in 1791*:

> The mansion of Colonel Wyllys I admired and the manners of the Colonel's family combined urbanity with dignity. The tea was served from trays, in a large room—a room much larger than was common at that age. The service was more splendid than I had before seen. It stood under the mahogany table,—it was the fashion, then. A silver teakettle stood on a silver chafing-dish. Coal might be placed in the chafing-dish and that kept the water hot. A large tea-urn of silver and a silver waiter stood on the table, with a silver teapot, sugar dish and milk pot surrounded by an elegant set of china service. I had never seen so much silver service and it was regarded as an evidence of ancient wealth and family.

The teapot popular in Boston followed the contemporary English style and was elliptical in plan, with straight spout and sides: it was seamed at the handle, since by this period the silversmith could purchase rolled sheets, which while contributing to a lowering of the skill required in raising, also saved time and labor. The body was decorated with horizontal delicate bands of bright-cut floral or acorn patterns, whose shallow depth did not serve to weaken the thin walls of the teapot. The slightly domed engraved cover was surmounted by a finial usually in pine-cone form. The plain body was varied by the occasional use of shaped or fluted sides. In the case of the latter, the fluted surface is emphasized by engraved swags of tasselled drapery in the Adam style. For insulation purposes the teapot was usually accompanied by its footed tray. This shape was succeeded by an elliptical teapot with slightly curving sides and concave shoulder and was decorated with applied horizontal reeded bands and bright-cut ornament. The matching cream jug with a high, looped strap handle was of helmet shape with plain or fluted footed body resting usually on a square base. The sugar dish, inspired by the Roman funerary urn, had an ovoid footed body, square base and tall, conical, incurved cover with a pine cone or flame finial similar to the teapot. The footed, boat-shaped sugar basket, plain or fluted, with swinging bail handle also became popular in Revere's shop. A fluted tea service fashioned in 1792 by Revere contains in addition to the usual teapot and tray, cream jug, and sugar basin, a tea caddy (Minneapolis Institute of Art).

Typical of his later style is the three-piece presentation set of 1799, made to memorialize the launching of the frigate *Boston*, built with funds subscribed by the Bostonians and launched at Hartt's Naval Yard, June 12, 1799. The set is decorated with bright-cut floral bands, the recipient's monogram and, upon the teapot and sugar basin, this legend:

To/Edmund Hartt/Constructor of the Frigate BOSTON/Presented by a number of his fellow citizens as a/Memorial of their sense of his Ability, Zeal & Fidelity/in the Completion of that Ornament/of the AMERICAN NAVY/1799. [Museum of Fine Arts.]

The New York tea set, while following the classical style, has a more lavish engraved ornament of pendent garlands with rim and base lines emphasized by beaded bands. One local feature is the rounded domed cover of the sugar basin surmounted by a cast finial in the shape of an acorn or a pineapple, symbol of hospitality. This is illustrated in a set by Ephraim Brasher, famous for minting the Brasher Doubloon in 1786, a gold coin now extremely rare. On the whole, New York hollow-ware in this period lacks the balance and proportion found in the other centers.

Philadelphia, convention city of the Continental Congress, and seat of the Federal Government, 1790–1800, developed a local style characterized by the use of a pierced gallery on the rims of sugar basin, teapot, coffee pot and even waste bowl, possibly inspired by the pierced edges of imported Sheffield trays. The popularity of Sheffield plate in Philadelphia by 1797 warranted George and Robert Armitage from Sheffield, in Europe, to establish themselves as "Manufacturers of Silver and Plated Tea and Tables Equipage." The urn-shaped bodies of the sugar basin and teapot are often plain, enriched only with finely cast beaded mouldings, with urn or pineapple finials on the tall domed incurved covers. The helmet cream jug is sometimes found with a cover. For variety, the bodies are placed diagonally on the square base, as in a set (Plate 28) fashioned by Abraham Dubois for Vice-President Aaron Burr (Garvan Collection). The elliptical straight-sided teapot and stand is also found with the drum shape from the previous period modernized by means of a classical pineapple finial. The rare locking tea caddy follows the same form and decoration as the teapot. The highly polished surface found on much of the silver produced here from 1790 to 1800 suggests a difference in standards. This is further indicated by Joseph Cooke's advertisement of 1795 offering "Sideboards and tea sets of plate, made of silver equal to dollars, burnished, and not inferior in workmanship to any from Europe, 15s. per oz. for silver and making; high polished do. made of British standard, 18s. 9d."

The continued use of the inverted pear form for the coffee pot is found in Boston, New York, Philadelphia, Annapolis, Baltimore and Charleston. The only concessions made to the classical style are the single scrolled wooden handle and bright-cut decoration. In Philadelphia one also finds the urn-shaped coffee pot. This shape, adapted from the Sheffield plated "Adam jug" pattern was employed by Revere for church flagons in the 1790's, a late instance of the influence of the shape of domestic upon ecclesiastical silver.

Imposing spouted urns for coffee and tea are among the new forms introduced in this period. Of the three surviving examples by Revere, one recorded in 1793 is fluted, two are plain. Rich in historic interest is the urn with plain ovoid body, square base, ball and claw feet, tall incurved conical cover and high looped handles (Plate 29), which was fashioned in 1800, according to its legend,

To/PERPETUATE/the Gallant defense/MADE BY/CPA[t] GAMALIEL BRADFORD/in the Ship Industry on the 8th July 1800/when attacked by four French Privateers/in the Streights of Gibraltar/This URN is presented to him/by/SAMUEL PARKMAN. [Massachusetts Historical Society.]

Small circular salvers for coffee pots, with beaded mouldings, claw and ball feet, and bright-cut engraving are found along with large oval footless salvers with handles, for tea sets and tumblers; and one advertisement offers "waiters holding from three to twelve glasses." Perhaps such was the purpose of the "waiter," recorded by Revere in his account book in 1797, fashioned for Salem's affluent merchant, Elias Hasket Derby, whose house and furnishings were famous in their day. Oval in plan, with moulded scalloped rim, enriched with shells and two angular bail handles, it remains one of Revere's masterpieces, and a relic of Salem's period of great prosperity (Garvan Collection).

Urn-shaped pepper castors with flame finials and delicate bright-cut decoration are found in company with oval pierced glass-lined salts. Joseph Anthony, Jr., advertised in Philadelphia in 1790 "a few blue glasses for salts." Glass was also used as a liner for mustard pots, or "mustard tankards" as they were termed in contemporary lists. An elliptical pierced and engraved example (from Philadelphia by an unidentified S.S.) having a domed cover, urn finial and blue glass liner, and a plain circular covered one, glass-lined and with spoon, made by Revere for Elias Hasket Derby, are contained in the Garvan Collection.

A boat-shaped body on oval foot, with loop handles or hanging rings, was popular for salts and covered sauce tureens, the successors of the sauce boats. A unique covered soup tureen of generous proportions was fashioned in this style by Charles Louis Boehme, one of the leading Baltimore silversmiths (Mrs. Miles White, Jr., Collection, Baltimore

Museum of Art). The popularity of this shape in Baltimore silver is further evidenced by the surviving cake baskets with swinging bail handles, ornamented with delicate bright-cut designs.

There is a noticeable similarity between the silver of Philadelphia and Baltimore in the last decade of the period. This is due partly to the fact that a great number of Philadelphia craftsmen settled in Baltimore following the disastrous yellow fever epidemics of 1793 and 1798 and the removal of the National Capitol to Washington in June 1800. By the following decade Baltimore silver had developed, in its use of rich bands of bright-cut ornament, effectively placed, a distinctive style comparable to its school of cabinet-making.

Examples of candlesticks, circular or oval in plan with moulded bases and nozzles, plain or decorated with a stamped design featuring an Adam sunburst on the base, have also been found. Made of thin silver and seamed, they are often weighted with pitch, like the contemporary Sheffield plated candlesticks. The chamber candlestick with urn-shaped candle socket, conical extinguisher and scissor-snuffer in a boat-shaped tray, executed by Joseph Lownes, is one of the most delightful pieces in this style on loan at the Philadelphia Museum of Art.

Small personal accessories surviving from the period include snuff boxes, shoe and knee buckles, thimbles, scissor chains, pincushion-hoops and chains, in silver, as well as gold rings, sleeve buttons, buckles, beads, chains and cases for miniature likenesses, then at the height of their vogue. Many a Federal goldsmith's work has survived as a setting for the artistic triumphs of Joseph Dunkerley, Robert Field, Edward Greene Malbone, James Peale and John Ramage.

Among the pieces officially commissioned during this period are the oval engraved Peace Medals presented to ranking Indian chieftains with great ceremony upon the occasion of diplomatic visits to the "Great White Father" (Plate 30). Engraved on the obverse is an Indian chief wearing a peace medal, standing before a pine tree, with a discarded tomahawk on the ground; he is smoking a peace pipe that has been presented to him by Washington in military uniform. Behind them in the distant fields a farmer is plowing with a yoke of oxen above the inscription "GEORGE WASHINGTON/PRESIDENT 1793"; on the reverse is the arms of the United States (Mark Bortman Collection). Of the surviving medals dating from 1792, 1793, 1795, a few of 1793 and all of 1795 are the work of Joseph Richardson, Jr. (1752–1831), who was appointed an assayer of the U.S. Mint by President Washington in 1795.

Other official pieces include two oval gold boxes, engraved with a bright-cut border and the arms of New York City, presented with the freedom of the city in October, 1784, to John Jay and Major General "Baron de Steuben." Made by Samuel Johnson, they were engraved by Peter Maverick, a prominent engraver in his day, and remain the earliest dated example of bright-cut engraving that has been noted. The Jay box is still owned by the family; the other is in the Garvan Collection (Plate III). Three other gold boxes ordered at the same time for presentation to Governor George Clinton, the Marquis de Lafayette and General Washington are recorded, but have not been located. Of greater historic interest is the small gold urn with reeded moulding, conical incurved cover and circular foot, fashioned in 1800 by Paul Revere to contain the lock of Washington's hair presented to the Grand Lodge of Massachusetts. A perfect example of the most appropriate use of the classical funerary urn, it is still preserved among the treasures of the Grand Lodge.

Appropriateness of form to function was not so carefully observed in the decade following Washington's death. A desire for novelty in a reaction against the reserve of the forms of classic inspiration led to the use for pouring vessels of the boat-shape on oval foot, which had been appropriate for standing containers such as tureens and salts. The resulting tea, coffee, and hot water pots in this style are ungainly, tending towards the heaviness that characterizes the succeeding period.

One of the most charming aspects in the field of engraving is the delightful execution of floriate monograms or cyphers within a bright-cut design. Its enclosure with bow-knotted ribbons and crossed wheat ears is characteristic of Philadelphia, where Joseph Cooke advertised in 1789: "The Initials of any Person's name, in a cypher, engraved after the famous Lockington's London Patent cypher-book."

Heraldic engraving in this period suffers from the discipline of classic form. It is usually displayed in a heart-shaped shield, similar to the Hepplewhite chair back, sometimes with suspended floral garlands on either side, or in an oval, bright-cut medallion suspended from ribbons as in the Bleecker arms on a ewer by Isaac Hutton (Garvan Collection). Stark though it is in its simplicity, one misses the beautifully executed mantling or cartouches of the earlier periods. The continued interest expressed in heraldry in the early years of the federal period and the arguments in its favor as set forth in 1785 by the persuasive Thomas Reynolds of Dublin are sufficiently pertinent to warrant inclusion:

To the Public. The Subscriber, in the course of his business, in their country as a Seal-Cutter, has had frequent occasion to observe the difficulty to which Gentlemen are liable here, in ascertaining and procuring the Armorial Bearings of their families, owing to their distance from the usual sources of information and other causes arising from thence. The principal Use of Coats of Arms, is to serve as markes of insignia, and to distinguish the different Families of a country, and to distinguish between those of the same name but different family. Considering them in this point of view, it must be evident, that in the present infant state of this independent empire, if its inhabitants were to pay attention to the attaining and preserving of their family arms, they might be made subservient to the valuable purpose of ascertaining descents, perpetuating the memorial of kindred by marriage, and pointing to the various branches of the same family, however numerous or remote. The above considerations have induced the subscriber at a considerable expense and trouble, to provide himself with a most expencive and curious collection of Coats of Arms, and Books of Heraldry he therefore proposes to supply those who apply to him from any part of the continent, with their Arms, truly and properly blazoned, at four dollars each; one dollar to be paid previous to the search, and the remainder on delivery of the Arms. Such arms as the subscriber cannot find in his collection shall be sent for to Europe, as he has established large connections in the Heraldry line, in different parts. To defray the charges thereof, the deposit of one dollar is required; yet should he finally prove unsuccessful, the money shall be returned. All persons applying, shall have their arms, names, and places of abode, registered in a regular book kept for that purpose. Coats of Arms, Cyphers, Crests, and all sorts of Devices cut in the newest Style.

N.B. An apprentice of genteel connections wanted.—Thomas Reynolds—*Freeman's Journal*, June 1–15, 1785.

REVERE

Chapter seven

The Vagaries of 19th-Century Taste

THE WIDESPREAD INTEREST IN ARCHAEOLOGY, STIMULATED BY THE excavations at Herculaneum and Pompeii, that was responsible for the beginning of the classical revival soon turned to Egypt and Greece, with the result that the new styles were based upon Greek and Egyptian ornament. The Greek War for Independence in the Byron-reading world of the 1820's ushered in a mania for things Greek which spread to architecture, furniture, silver and even dress. But being revivals, these fashions were quick to come and quick to go. Increased travel in the Orient and the popularity of travel books were responsible by 1850 for a wave of Persian and Turkish modes in architecture and the decorative arts.

The increased use of the machine, and the development of specialization of labor following the industrial revolution are largely to blame for the lack of harmony between form and function in mid-nineteenth-century silver. Unlike the practice in the days of Coney or Revere, designs were largely drawn by artists who had little or no idea of the material in which these designs were to be executed, with a resultant loss in appropriateness and proportion.

Flatware reflects these changing fashions less than other ware. The spoon, slightly larger in all sizes, changes from the rounded and coffin-end handle of 1810 to a plain, spatulate, usually down-curved handle

Plate 31

Philip Garrett's tea caddy of 1817 demonstrates in its engraved ornament an early instance of the coarsening of classical ornament occurring in the first quarter of the 19th century. Height 9½″

The influence of French Empire style is naively expressed by Harvey Lewis of Philadelphia in this inkstand in which the supporting French sphinxes are transmogrified, by the addition of feathers, into redskins. Height $3\frac{7}{16}$"

commonly referred to as "fiddle," occasionally decorated on the handle end with a stamped design of a floral basket, wheatsheaf or shell in relief. This remained in vogue until the 1830's, when it was succeeded by a spatulate, up-curved handle, thickened at the end, and by the mid-century this in turn was replaced by a variety of fairly simple patterns stamped from machine dies (Plate 2b).

Classically inspired shapes in hollow-ware persisted until 1820 but one notices a coarsening in the scale of ornament, first expressed in the bright-cut design, as in the broad bands on the tea caddy (Plate 31) made by Philip Garrett in 1817 (Garvan Collection). Their falling into the discard was partly due to the popularity of the French Empire style, generally expressed in America following the War of 1812, in banded laurel ornament and sphinx supports. A charmingly naïve expression of this influence is to be found in an inkstand (Plate 32) fashioned *c.*1815 by Harvey Lewis, on which the supports of the ink bowl are winged sphinxes transmogrified into Redskins (Garvan Collection).

Contemporary with these are occasional pieces which in harmony of design, proportion and craftsmanship, are worthy of the earlier traditions. Excellent examples of this are the plain low circular pudding dishes, inspired by ceramic form, to which the silversmith has added a charming scalloped rim, fashioned by Shepherd and Boyd in Albany in 1815 for the Van Cortlandt family; there are other admirable examples in the surviving pieces by their contemporaries, Isaac Hutton, or Bostonian Obadiah Rich.

After 1820, hollow-ware on the whole was much larger, circular or polygonal in plan and was decorated with enlarged broad gadrooning, applied stamped or chased bands of heavy ornament, ranging from laurel wreaths, Greek water leaves, roses or grapevines to rustic scenes of wandering milkmaids, cows and windmills. The favored supports were large ball feet and the winged claw feet seen on late Phyfe furniture. Handle designs ranged from the simple scroll to those simulating tree branches, grapevines, or ramsheads; finials ranged from roses or vegetables to Chinese coolies, as on teapots by R. & W. Wilson of Philadelphia. An all-over repoussé floral pattern, popularized in Baltimore in the nineteenth century by Samuel Kirk, is associated with that firm's silver from 1830 to the present day. Conspicuously absent is the tankard, and many of the earlier ones unfortunately had their original shapes distorted by the addition of a spout, largely traceable to the burgeoning temperance movement of the first quarter of the nineteenth century.

As this era of expansion progressed, the shapes increased in size, variety and decoration, as exemplified in a presentation service numbering nearly 400 pieces fashioned at a cost of $6,000 by William Gale in 1855 as a gift from the Chamber of Commerce and the merchants of New York to Commodore Matthew C. Perry, U.S.N., in recognition of his services in concluding the U.S.-Japanese treaty of 1854 (New York Historical Society).

The low ebb of taste in American silver, as in architecture and furniture, appears to have been reached in 1876, judging by the catalog of the Centennial Exhibition. Typical in the catalog is a Reed and Barton tipping water pitcher; it rides on wheels and its surface is nowhere free from unrestrained jungle masses of naturalistic forms in chasing and repoussé, a far cry from the functional simplicity of the water pitcher of Paul Revere.

The revival of craftsmanship in silver during the past thirty years is largely due to the efforts of skilled artisans trained by early apprenticeship methods. It is unfortunate that their craftsmanship, largely conditioned by patronage, has been restricted mainly to copies of, or designs based on, early styles. One of the great charms of the silver of the seventeenth and eighteenth centuries, in addition to the necessary attributes of appropriateness of form, lies in its expression of contemporary life. It is still to be hoped that an era in which such progress has been made in science, medicine, architecture, the machine, moving pictures and radio can evolve a style in silver that two hundred years hence will be as expressive of our time as John Hull's silver is of his.

WISHART

Bibliography

HISTORY AND STYLE

Avery, C. L. *Early American Silver.* 1930.

Bigelow, F. H. *Historic Silver of the Colonies and its Makers.* 1917.

Buck, J. H. *Old Plate, its Makers and Marks.* 1903.

Burton, E. Milby. *South Carolina Silversmiths 1690–1860.* 1942.

Curtis, G. M. *Early Silver of Connecticut and Its Makers.* 1913.

Jones, E. A. *The Old Silver of American Churches.* 1913.

Jones, E. A. *Old Silver of Europe and America.* 1928.

Pleasants, G. Hall, and Sill, Howard. *Maryland Silversmiths 1715–1830.* 1930.

MARKS

Brix, M. *List of Philadelphia Silversmiths and Allied Artificers from 1682–1850.* 1920.

Currier, E. M. *Marks of Early American Silversmiths.* 1938.

Ensko, S. G. *American Silversmiths and their Marks.* 1927.

Ensko, S. G. *American Silversmiths and their Marks, No. III.* 1948.

French, H. *A List of Early American Silversmiths and their Marks.* 1917.

Graham, J., Jr. *Early American Silver Marks.* 1936.

PUBLIC COLLECTIONS IN

Albany, N.Y. Albany Institute of History and Art

Andover, Mass. Addison Gallery of American Art, Phillips Academy

Baltimore, Md. Baltimore Museum of Art

Boston, Mass. Museum of Fine Arts

Cambridge, Mass. William Hayes Fogg Museum of Art

Chicago, Ill. Art Institute of Chicago

Cleveland, Ohio. Cleveland Museum of Art

Detroit, Mich. Detroit Institute of Arts

Minneapolis, Minn. Minneapolis Institute of Arts

New Haven, Conn. Yale University Art Gallery

New York, N.Y. Metropolitan Museum of Art, Museum of the City of New York, NewYork Historical Society

Philadelphia, Pa. Historical Society of Pennsylvania, Philadelphia Museum of Art

Providence, Rhode Island. Rhode Island School of Design

St. Louis, Mo. City Art Museum

Worcester, Mass. Worcester Art Museum

Ram's horn thumbpiece from a William and Mary tankard